Nora Archibald Smith, Kate Douglas Smith Wiggin

The Story Hour

A Book for the Home and the Kindergarten

Nora Archibald Smith, Kate Douglas Smith Wiggin

The Story Hour
A Book for the Home and the Kindergarten

ISBN/EAN: 9783337241070

Printed in Europe, USA, Canada, Australia, Japan

Cover: Foto ©ninafisch / pixelio.de

More available books at **www.hansebooks.com**

THE STORY HOUR

A BOOK FOR THE HOME AND THE KINDERGARTEN

BY

KATE DOUGLAS WIGGIN

AND

NORA A. SMITH

Therefore ear and heart open to the genuine story-teller as flowers open to the spring sun and the May rain.
FRIEDRICH FROEBEL

BOSTON AND NEW YORK
HOUGHTON MIFFLIN COMPANY
The Riverside Press Cambridge

Copyright, 1890,
By KATE DOUGLAS WIGGIN AND NORA A. SMITH

All rights reserved.

CONTENTS.

INTRODUCTION. *Kate Douglas Wiggin* 5
PREFACE. *Kate Douglas Wiggin* and *Nora A. Smith* . . 27
THE ORIOLE'S NEST. *Kate Douglas Wiggin* 29
DICKY SMILEY'S BIRTHDAY. *Kate Douglas Wiggin* . . 38
AQUA; OR, THE WATER BABY. *Kate Douglas Wiggin* . 52
MOUFFLOU. Adapted from Ouida by *Nora A. Smith* . . 59
BENJY IN BEASTLAND. Adapted from Mrs. Ewing by *Kate Douglas Wiggin* and *Nora A. Smith* 72
THE PORCELAIN STOVE. Adapted from Ouida by *Kate Douglas Wiggin* 83
THE BABES IN THE WOOD. *E. S. Smith* 96
THE STORY OF CHRISTMAS. *Nora A. Smith* 101
THE FIRST THANKSGIVING DAY. *Nora A. Smith* . . . 107
LITTLE GEORGE WASHINGTON. Part I. *Nora A. Smith* . 115
GREAT GEORGE WASHINGTON. Part II. *Nora A. Smith* 123
THE MAPLE-LEAF AND THE VIOLET. *Nora A. Smith* . 133
MRS. CHINCHILLA. *Kate Douglas Wiggin* 139
A STORY OF THE FOREST. *Nora A. Smith* 146
PICCOLA. *Nora A. Smith* 156
THE CHILD AND THE WORLD. *Kate Douglas Wiggin* . . 165
WHEN I WAS A LITTLE GIRL. *Kate Douglas Wiggin* . 168
FROEBEL'S BIRTHDAY. *Nora A. Smith* 179

INTRODUCTION.

STORY-TELLING, like letter-writing, is going out of fashion. There are no modern Scheherezades, and the Sultans nowadays have to be amused in a different fashion. But, for that matter, a hundred poetic pastimes of leisure have fled before the relentless Hurry Demon who governs this prosaic nineteenth century. The Wandering Minstrel is gone, and the Troubadour, and the Court of Love, and the King's Fool, and the Round Table, and with them the Story-Teller.

"Come, tell us a story!" It is the familiar plea of childhood. Unhappy he who has not been assailed with it again and again. Thrice miserable she who can be consigned to worse than oblivion by the scathing criticism, "She does n't know any stories!" and thrice blessed she who is recognized at a glance as a person likely to be full to the brim of them.

There are few preliminaries and no formalities when the Person with a Story is found.

The motherly little sister stands by the side of her chair, two or three of the smaller fry perch on the arms, and the baby climbs up into her lap (such a person always has a capacious lap), and folds his fat hands placidly. Then there is a deep sigh of blissful expectation and an expressive silence, which means, "Now we are ready, please; and if you would be kind enough to begin it with 'Once upon a time,' we should be much obliged; though of course we understand that all the stories in the world can't commence that way, delightful as it would be."

The Person with a Story smiles obligingly (at least it is to be hoped that she does), and retires into a little corner of her brain, to rummage there for something just fitted to the occasion. That same little corner is densely populated, if she is a lover of children. In it are all sorts of heroic dogs, wonderful monkeys, intelligent cats, naughty kittens; virtues masquerading seductively as fairies, and vices hiding in imps; birds agreeing and disagreeing in their little nests, and inevitable small boys in the act of robbing them; busy bees laying up their winter stores, and idle butterflies disgracefully neglecting to do the same; and then a troop of lost children, disobedient children, and lazy, industrious, generous, or heedless ones, waiting to furnish the thrilling climaxes. The Story-Teller selects a hero or heroine out of this motley crowd, — all longing to be introduced to Bright-Eye, Fine-Ear, Kind-Heart, and Sweet-Lips, — and speedily the drama opens.

Did Rachel ever have such an audience? I trow not. Rachel never had tiny hands snuggling into hers in " the very best part of the story," nor was she near enough her hearers to mark the thousand shades of expression that chased each other across their faces, — supposing they had any expression, which is doubtful. Rachel never saw dimples lurking in the ambush of rosy cheeks, and popping in and out in such a distracting manner that she felt like punctuating her discourse with kisses! Her dull, conventional, grown-up hearers bent a little forward in their seats, perhaps, and compelled by her magic power laughed and cried in the right places; but their eyes never shone with that starry lustre that we see in the eyes of happy children, —

a lustre that is dimmed, alas, in after years. Their eyes still see visions, but the "shadows of the prison house" have fallen about us, and the things which we have seen we "now can see no more!"

If you chance to be the Person with a Story, you sit like a queen on her throne surrounded by her loyal subjects; or like an unworthy sun with a group of flowers turning their faces towards you. Inspired by breathless attention, you try ardently to do your very best. It seems to you that you could never endure a total failure, and you hardly see how you could bear, with any sort of equanimity, even the vacant gaze or restless movement that would bespeak a vagrant interest. If you are a novice, perhaps the frightful idea crosses your mind, "What if one of these children should slip out of the room?" Or, still more tragic possibility, suppose they should look you in the eye and remark with the terrible candor of infancy, "We do not like this story!" But no; you are more fortunate. The tale is told, and you are greeted with sighs of satisfaction and with the instantaneous request, "Tell it again!" That is the encore of the Story-Teller, — "Tell it again! No, not another story; the same one over again, please!" for "what novelty is worth that sweet monotony where everything is known, and loved because it is known?" No royal accolade could be received with greater gratitude. You endeavor to let humility wait upon self-respect; but when you discover that the children can scarcely be dragged from your fascinating presence, crying like Romeo for death rather than banishment, and that the next time you appear they make a wild dash from the upper regions, and precipitate themselves upon you with the full impact of their several weights "multiplied into their velocity," you cannot help hugging yourself to think the good God has endowed you sufficiently to win the love and admiration of such keen observers and merciless little critics.

Now this charming little drama takes place in somebody's nursery corner at twilight, when you are waiting for "that cheerful tocsin of the soul, the dinner-bell," or around somebody's fireside just before the children's bedtime; but the same scene is enacted every few days in the presence of the fresh-hearted, childlike kindergartner, of all women the likeliest to find the secret of eternal youth. She chooses the story as one of the vessels in which she shall carry the truth to her circle of little listeners, and you will never hear her say, like the needy knife-grinder, "Story? God bless you, I have none to tell, sir!"

If the group chances to be one of bright, well-born, well-bred youngsters, the opportunity to inspire and instruct is one of the most effective and valuable that can come to any teacher. On the other hand, if the circle happens to be one of little ragamuffins, Arabs, scrips and scraps of vagrant humanity (sometimes scalawags and sometimes angels), born in basements and bred on curbstones, then believe me, my countrymen, there is a sight worth seeing, a scene fit for a painter. It might be a pleasant satire upon our national hospitality if the artist were to call such a picture "Young America," for comparatively few distinctively American faces would be found in his group of portraits.

Make a mental picture, dear reader, of the ring of listening children in a San Francisco free kindergarten, for it would be difficult to gather so cosmopolitan a company anywhere else: curly yellow hair and rosy cheeks . . . sleek blonde braids and calm blue eyes . . . swarthy faces and blue-black curls . . . woolly little pows and thick lips . . . long, arched noses and broad, flat ones. There you will see the fire and passion of the Southern races and the self-poise, serenity, and sturdiness of Northern nations. Pat is there, with a gleam of humor in his eye . . . Topsy, all smiles and teeth . . . Abraham, trading tops with little Isaac, next in line . . . Hans and Gretchen, phlegmatic and dependable . . . François, never still for an instant . . . Christina, rosy, calm, and conscientious, and Duncan, canny and prudent as any of his clan.

What an opportunity for amalgamation of races and for laying the foundation of American citizenship! for the purely social atmosphere of the kindergarten makes it a school of life and experience. Imagine such a group hanging breathless upon your words, as you recount the landing of the Pilgrims, or try to paint the character of George Washington in colors that shall appeal to children whose ancestors have known Napoleon, Cromwell, and Bismarck, Peter the Great, Garibaldi, Bruce, and Robert Emmett.

To such an audience were the stories in this little book told; and the lines that will perhaps seem commonplace to you glow for us with a "light that never was on sea or land;" for "the secret of our emotions never lies in the bare object, but in its subtle relations to our own past."

As we turn the pages, radiant faces peep between the words; the echo of childish laughter rings in our ears and curves our lips with its happy memory; there isn't a single round O in all the chapters but serves as a tiny picture-frame for an eager child's face! The commas say, "Isn't there any more?" the interrogation points ask, "What did the boy do then?" the exclamation points cry in ecstasy, "What a beautiful story!" and the periods sigh, "This is all for to-day."

At this point — where the dog Moufflou returns to his little master — we remember that Carlotty Griggs clapped her ebony hands, and shrieked in transport, "I *knowed* he'd come! *I knowed* he'd come!"

INTRODUCTION. 13

Here is the place where we remarked impressively, "A lie, children, is the very worst thing in the world!" whereupon Billy interrogated, with wide eyes and awed voice, "*Is it worse than a railroad crossing?*" And there is a sentence in the story of the "Bird's Nest" sacred to the memory of Tommy's tear! — Tommy of the callous conscience and the marble heart. Tommy's dull eye washed for one brief moment by the salutary tear! Truly the humble Story-Teller has not lived in vain. Sing, ye morning stars, together, for this is the spot where Tommy cried!

If you would be the Person with a Story, you must not only have one to tell, but you must be willing to learn how to tell it, if you wish to make it a "rememberable thing" to children. The Story-Teller, unlike the poet, is made as well as born, but he is not made of all stuffs nor in the twinkling of an eye. In this respect he is very like the Ichneumon in the nonsense rhyme: —

"There once was an idle Ichneumon
Who thought he could learn to play Schumann;
But he found, to his pains,
It took talent and brains,
And neither possessed this Ichneumon."

To be effective, the story in the kindergarten should always be told, never read; for little children need the magnetism of eye and smile as well as the gesture which illuminates the strange word and endows it with meaning. The story that is told is always a thousand times more attractive, real, and personal than anything read from a book.

Well-chosen, graphically told stories can be made of distinct educative value in the nursery or kindergarten. They give the child a love of reading, develop in him the germ, at least, of a taste for good literature, and teach him the art of speech. If they are told in simple, graceful, expressive English, they are a direct and valuable object lesson in this last direction.

The ear of the child becomes used to refined intonations, and slovenly language will grow more and more disagreeable to him. The kindergartner cannot be too careful in this matter. By the sweetness of her tone and the perfection of her enunciation she not only makes herself a worthy model for the children, but she constantly reveals the possibilities of language and its inner meaning.

"The very brooding of a voice on a word," says George Macdonald, " seems to hatch something of what is in it."

Stories help a child to form a standard by which he can live and grow, for they are his first introduction into the grand world of the ideal in character.

> "We live by Admiration, Hope, and Love;
> And even as these are well and wisely fixed,
> In dignity of being we ascend."

The child understands his own life better, when he is enabled to compare it with other lives; he sees himself and his own possibilities reflected in them as in a mirror.

They also aid in the growth of the imaginative faculty, which is very early developed in the child, and requires its natural food. "Imagination," says Dr. Seguin, "is more than a decorative attribute of leisure; it is a power in the sense that from images perceived and stored it sublimes ideals." "If I were to choose between two great calamities for my children," he goes on to say, "I would rather have them unalphabetic than unimaginative."

There is a great difference of opinion concerning the value of fairy stories. The Gradgrinds will not accept them on any basis whatever, but they are invariably so fascinating to children that it is certain they must serve some good purpose and appeal to some inherent craving in child-nature. But here comes in the necessity of discrimination. The true meaning of the word "faerie" is spiritual, but many stories masquerade under that title which have no claim to it. Some universal spiritual truth underlies the really fine old fairy tale; but there can be no educative influence in the so-called fairy stories which are merely jumbles of impossible incidents, and which not unfrequently present dishonesty, deceit, and cruelty in attractive or amusing guise.

When the fairy tale carries us into an exquisite ideal world, where the fancy may roam at will, creating new images and seeing truth ever in new forms, then it has a pure and lovely influence over children, who are natural poets, and live more in the spirit and less in the body than we. The fairy tale offers us a broad canvas on which to paint our word-pictures. There are no restrictions of time or space; the world is ours, and we can roam in it at will; for spirit, there, is ever victorious over matter.

"Once upon a time," saith the Story-Teller, "there was a beautiful locust tree, that bent its delicate fans and waved its creamy blossoms in the sunshine, and laughed because its flowers were so lovely and fragrant and the world was so fresh and green in its summer dress."

"It's queer for a tree to laugh," said Bright-Eye.

"But queerer if it did n't laugh, with such lovely blossoms hanging all over it," replied Fine-Ear.

Everything is real to the happy child. Life is a sort of fairy garden, where he wanders as in a dream. "He can make abstraction of whatever does not fit into his fable; and he puts his eyes into his pocket just as we hold our noses in an unsavory lane."

Stories offer a valuable field for instruction, and for introducing in simple and attractive form much information concerning the laws of plant and flower and animal life.

A story of this kind, however, must be

made as well as told by an artist; for in the hands of a bungler it is quite as likely to be a failure as a success. It must be compounded with the greatest care, and the scientific facts must be generously diluted and mixed in small proportions with other and more attractive elements, or it will be rejected by the mental stomach; or, if received in one ear, will be unceremoniously ushered from the other with an "Avaunt! cold fact! What have thou and I in common!"

Did you ever tell a story of this kind and watch its effect upon children? Did you ever note that fatal moment when it *began to begin* to dawn upon the intelligence of the dullest member of your flock that your narrative was a "whited sepulchre," and that he was being instructed within an inch of his life?

"Treat me at least with honesty, my good woman!" he cries in his spirit. "Read me lessons if you will, but do not make a pretense of amusing me at the same moment!"

This obvious attitude of criticism is very disagreeable to you, but never mind, it will be a salutary lesson. Did you think, O clumsy visitor in childhood land, that simply because you called your stuffed dolls "Prince" and "Princess" you could conduct them straight through the mineral kingdom, and allow them to converse with all the metals with impunity? Next time make your scientific fact an integral part of the story, and do not try to introduce too much knowledge in one dose. All children love Nature and sympathize with her (or if they do not, "then despair of them, O Philanthropy!"), and all stories that bring them nearer to the dear mother's heart bring them at the same time nearer to God; therefore lead them gently to a loving observation of

> "The hills
> Rock-ribbed and ancient as the sun; the vales
> Stretching in pensive quietness between;
> The venerable woods; rivers that move
> In majesty, and the complaining brooks
> That make the meadows green."

Stories bring the force of example to bear upon children in the very best possible way. Here we can speak to the newly awakened soul and touch it to nobler issues. This can be done with very little of that abstract moralizing which is generally so ineffective. A moral "lugged in" by the heels, so to speak, without any sense of perspective on the part of the Story-Teller, can no more incline a child to nobler living than cold victuals can serve as a fillip to the appetite. The facts themselves should suffice to exert the moral influence; the deeds should speak louder than the words, and in clearer, fuller tones. At the end of such a story, "Go thou and do likewise" sounds in the child's heart, and a new throb of tenderness and aspiration, of desire to do, to grow, and to be, stirs gently there and wakes the soul to higher ideals. In such a story the canting, vapid, or didactic little moral, tacked like a tag on the end, for fear we shall not read the lesson aright, is nothing short of an insult to the better feelings. It used to be very much in vogue, but we have learned better nowadays, and we recognize (to paraphrase Mrs. Whitney's bright speech) that we have often vaccinated children with morality for fear of their taking it the natural way.

It is a curious fact that children sympathize with the imaginary woes of birds and butterflies and plants much more readily than with the sufferings of human beings; and they are melted to tears much more quickly by simple incidents from the manifold life of nature, than by the tragedies of human experience which surround them on every side. Robert Louis Stevenson says in his essay on "Child's Play," "Once, when I was groaning aloud with physical pain, a young gentleman came into the room and nonchalantly inquired if I had seen his bow and arrow. He made no account of my groans, which he accepted, as he had to accept so much else, as a piece of the inexplicable conduct of his elders. Those elders, who care so little for rational enjoyment, and are even the enemies of rational enjoyment for others, he had accepted without understanding and without complaint, as the rest of us accept the scheme of the universe." Miss Anna Buckland quotes in this connection a story of a little boy to whom his mother showed a picture of Daniel in the lions' den. The child sighed and looked much distressed, whereupon his mother hastened to assure him that Daniel was such a good man that God did not let the lions hurt him. "Oh," replied the little fellow, "I was not thinking of that; but I was afraid that those big lions were going to eat all of him themselves, and that they would not give the poor little lion down in the corner any of him!"

It is well to remember the details with which you surrounded your story when first you told it, and hold to them strictly on all other occasions. The children allow you no latitude in this matter; they draw the line absolutely upon all change. Woe unto you, scribes and Pharisees, if you speak of Jimmy when "his name was Johnny;" or if, when you are depicting the fearful results of disobedience, you lose Jane in a cranberry bog instead of the heart of a forest! Personally you do not care much for little Jane, and it is a matter of no moment to you where you lost her; but an error such as this undermines the very foundations of the universe in the children's minds. "Can Jane be lost in two places?" they exclaim mentally, "or are there two Janes, and are they both lost? because if so, it must be a fatality to be named Jane."

Perez relates the following incident: "A certain child was fond of a story about a young bird, which, having left its nest, although its mother had forbidden it to do so, flew to the top of a chimney, fell down the flue into the fire, and died a victim to his disobedience. The person who told the story thought it necessary to embellish it from his own imagination. 'That's not right,' said the child at the first change which was made, 'the mother said this and did that.' His cousin, not remembering the story word for word, was obliged to have recourse to invention to fill up gaps. But the child could not stand it. He slid down from his cousin's knees, and with tears in his eyes, and indignant gestures, exclaimed, 'It's not true! The little bird said, *coui, coui, coui, coui*, before he fell into the fire, to make his mother hear; but the mother did not hear him, and he burnt his wings, his claws, and his beak, and he died, poor little bird.' And the child ran away, crying as if he had been beaten. He had been worse than beaten; he had been deceived, or at least he thought so; his story had been spoiled by being altered." So seriously do children for a long time take fiction for reality.

If you find the attention of the children wandering, you can frequently win it gently back by showing some object illustrative of your story, by drawing a hasty sketch on a blackboard, or by questions to the children. You sometimes receive more answers than you bargained for; sometimes these answers will be confounded with the real facts; and sometimes they will fall very wide of the mark.

I was once telling the exciting tale of the Shepherd's Child lost in the mountains, and of the sagacious dog who finally found him. When I reached the thrilling episode of the search, I followed the dog as he started from the shepherd's hut with the bit of breakfast for his little master. The shepherd sees the faithful creature, and seized by a sudden inspiration follows in his path. Up, up the mountain sides they climb, the father full of hope, the mother trembling with fear. The dog rushes ahead, quite out of sight; the anxious villagers press forward in hot pursuit. The situation grows more and more intense; they round a little point of rocks, and there, under the shadow of a great gray crag, they find —

"What do you suppose they found?"

"*Fi' cents!!*" shouted Benny in a transport of excitement. "*Bet yer they found fi' cents!!*"

You would imagine that such a preposterous idea could not find favor in any sane community; but so altogether seductive a guess did this appear to be, that a chorus of "Fi' cents!" "Fi' cents!" sounded on every side; and when the tumult was hushed, the discovery of an ordinary flesh and blood child fell like an anti-climax on a public thoroughly in love with its own incongruities. Let the psychologist explain Benny's mental processes; we prefer to leave them undisturbed and unclassified.

· · · · · · ·

If you have no children of your own, dear Person with a Story, go into the highways and by-ways and gather together the little ones whose mothers' lips are dumb; sealed by dull poverty, hard work, and constant life in atmospheres where graceful fancies are blighted as soon as they are born. There is no fireside, and no chimney corner in those crowded tenements. There is no silver-haired grandsire full of years and wisdom, with memory that runs back to the good old times that are no more. There is no cheerful grandame with pocket full of goodies and a store of dear old reminiscences all beginning with that enchanting phrase, "When I was a little girl."

Brighten these sordid lives a little with your pretty thoughts, your lovely imaginations, your tender pictures. Speak to them simply, for their minds grope feebly in the dim twilight of their restricted lives. The old, old stories will do; stories of love and heroism and sacrifice; of faith and courage and fidelity. Kindle in tired hearts a gentler thought of life; open the eyes that see not and the ears that hear not; interpret to them something of the beauty that has been revealed to you. You do not need talent, only sympathy, "the one poor word that includes all our best insight and our best love."

KATE DOUGLAS WIGGIN.

PREFACE.

The fourteen little stories in this book are not offered as a collection ample enough to satisfy all needs of the kindergartner.

Such a collection should embrace representative stories of all classes — narrative, realistic, imaginative, scientific, and historical, as well as brief and simple tales for the babies.

An experience of twelve years among kindergartners, however, has shown us that there is room for a number of books like this modest example; containing stories which need no adaptation or arrangement; which are ready for the occasion, and which have been thoroughly tried before audience after audience of children.

The three adaptations, "Benjy in Beast-Land," "Moufflou," and the "Porcelain

Stove," have been made as sympathetically as possible. Their introduction needs no apology, for they are exquisite stories, and in their original form much too advanced for children of the kindergarten age.

KATE DOUGLAS WIGGIN.
NORA A. SMITH.

THE ORIOLE'S NEST.

"See how each boy, excited by the actual event, is all ear." — FROEBEL.

THERE it hangs, on a corner of the picture frame, very much as it hung in the old willow-tree out in the garden.

It was spring time, and I used to move my rocking-chair up to the window, where I could lean out and touch the green branches, and watch there for the wonderful beautiful things to tell my little children in the kindergarten. There I saw the busy little ants hard at work on the ground below; the patient, dull, brown toads snapping flies in the sunshine; the striped caterpillars lazily crawling up the trunk of the tree; and dozens of merry birds getting ready for housekeeping.

Did you know the birdies "kept house"? Oh, yes; they never "board" like men and women; indeed, I don't think they even like to *rent* a house without fixing it over to suit themselves, but they'd much rather go to work and build one,

"So snug and so warm, so cosy and neat,
To start at their housekeeping all complete."

Now there hung just inside my window a box of strings, and for two or three days, no matter how many I put into it, when I went to look the next time none could be found. I had talked to the little girls and scolded the little boys in the house, but no one knew anything about the matter, when one afternoon, as I was sitting there, a beautiful bird with a yellow breast fluttered down from the willow-tree, perched on the window-sill, cocked his saucy head, winked his bright eye, and without saying "If you please," dipped his naughty little beak into the string box and flew off with a piece of pink twine.

I sat as still as a mouse to see if the little scamp would dare to come back; he did n't, but he sent his wife, who gave a hop, skip, and a jump, looked me squarely in the eye, and took her string without being a bit afraid.

Now do you call that stealing? "No," you answer. Neither do I; to be sure they took what belonged to me, but the window was wide open, and I think they must have known I loved the birds and would like to give them something for their new house. Perhaps they knew, too, that bits of old twine could not be worth much.

Then how busily they began their work! They had already chosen the place for their nest, springing up and down in the boughs till they found a branch far out of sight of snakes and hawks and cruel tabby cats, high out of reach of naughty small boys with their sling-shots, and now everything was ready for these small carpenters to begin their building. No hammer and nails were needed, claw and bill were all the tools they used, and yet what beautiful carpenter work was theirs!

Do you see how strongly the nest is tied on to those three slender twigs, and how carefully and closely it is woven, so that you can scarcely pull it apart?

Those wiry black hairs holding all the rest together were dropped from Prince Charming's tail (Prince Charming is the pretty saddle-horse who crops his grass under the willow-tree). Those sleek brown hairs belonged to Dame Margery, the gentle mooly cow, who lives with her little calf Pet in the stable with Prince Charming; and there is a shining yellow spot on one side. Ah, you roguish birds, you must have been outside the kitchen window when baby Johnny's curls were cut! We could only spare two from his precious head, and we hunted everywhere for this one to send to grandmamma!

Now just look at this door in the side of the nest, and tell me how a bird could make such a perfect one; and yet I've heard you say, "It's only a bird; he does n't know anything." To be sure he cannot do as many things as you, but after all you are not wise enough to do many of the things that he does. What would one of my little boys do, I wonder, if he were carried miles away from home and dropped in a place he had never seen? Why, he would be too frightened to do anything but cry; and yet there are many birds, who, when taken away a long distance, will perch on top of the weather-vane, perhaps, make up their little bits of minds which way to go, and then with a whir-r-r-r fly off over house-tops and church-steeples, towns and cities, rivers and meadows, until they reach the place from which they started.

Look at the nest for the last time now, and see the soft, lovely lining of ducks' feathers and lambs' wool.

Why do you suppose it was made so velvet soft and fleecy? Why, for the little birds that were coming, of course; and sure enough, one morning after the tiny house was all finished, I leaned far out of the window and saw five little eggs cuddled close together; but I did not get much chance to look at those precious eggs, I can tell you; for the mamma bird could scarcely spare a minute to go and get a drink of water, so afraid was she that they would miss the warmth of her downy wings.

There she sat in the long May days and warm, still nights: who but a mamma would be so sweet and kind and patient? — but *she* did n't mind the trouble — not a bit. Bless her dear little bird-heart, they were not eggs to her: she could see them even now as they were going to be, her five cunning, downy, feathery birdlings, chirping and fluttering under her wings; so she never minded the ache in her back or the cramp in her legs, but sat quite still at home, though there were splendid picnics in the strawberry patches and concerts on the fence rails, and all the father birds, and all the mother birds that were not hatching eggs, were having a great deal of fun this beautiful weather. At last all was over, and I was waked up one morning by such a chirping and singing — such a fluttering and flying — I knew in a minute that where the night before there had been two birds and five eggs, now there were seven birds and nothing but egg-shells in the green willow-tree!

The papa oriole would hardly wait for me to dress, but flew on and off the window-sill, seeming to say, "Why don't you get up? why don't you get up? I have five little birds; they came out of the shells this very morning, so hungry that I *can't* get enough for them to eat! Why don't you get up, I say? I have five little birds, and I am taking care of them while my wife is off taking a rest!"

They were five scrawny, skinny little things, I must say; for you know birds don't begin by being pretty like kittens and chickens, but look very bare and naked, and don't seem to have anything to show but a big, big mouth which is always opening and crying "Yip, yip, yip!"

Now I think you are wondering why I happen to have this nest, and how I could have taken away the beautiful house from the birds. Ah, that is the sad part of the story, and I wish I need not tell it to you.

When the baby birds were two days old, I went out on a long ride into the country, leaving everything safe and happy in the old green willow-tree; but when I came back, what do you think I found on the ground under the branches? —— —— A wonderful hangbird's nest cut from the tree, and five poor still birdies lying by its side. Five slender necks all limp and lifeless, — five pairs of bright eyes shut forever! and overhead the poor mamma and papa twittering and crying in the way little birds have when they are frightened and sorry — flying here and there, first down to the ground and then up in the tree, to see if it was really true.

While I was gone two naughty boys had

come into the garden to dig for angle-worms, and all at once they spied the oriole's nest.

"O Tommy, here's a hang-bird's nest, such a funny one! there's nobody here, let's get it," cried Jack.

Up against the tree they put the step-ladder, and although it was almost out of reach, a sharp jack-knife cut the twigs that held it up, and down it fell from the high tree with a heavy thud on the hard earth, and the five little orioles never breathed again! Of course the boys did n't know there were any birdies in the nest, or they would n't have done it for the world; but that did n't make it any easier for the papa and mamma bird.

Now, dear children, never let me hear you say, "It's no matter, they're only birds, they don't care."

Think about this nest: how the mother and father worked at it, weaving hair and string and wool together, day by day! Think how the patient mamma sat on the eggs, dreaming of the time when she should have five little singing, flying birds to care for, to feed and to teach! and then to have them live only two short days! Was it not dreadful to lose her beautiful house and dear little children both at once?

Never forget that just as your own father and mother love their dear little girls and boys, so God has made the birds love their little feathery children that are born in the wonderful nests he teaches them to build.

DICKY SMILEY'S BIRTHDAY.

"In order to be especially beneficial and effective, story-telling should be connected with the events and occurrences of life." — FROEBEL.

DICKY SMILEY was eight years old when all these things happened that I am going to tell you; eight years old, and as bright as a steel button. It was very funny that his name should be Smiley, for his face was just like a sunbeam, and if he ever cried at all it was only for a minute, and then the smiles would creep out and chase the tear-drops away from the blue sky of his eyes.

Dicky's mother tried to call him Richard, because it was his papa's name, but it never would say itself somehow, and even when she did remember, and called him "Richard," his baby sister Dot would cry, "Mamma, don't scold Dicky."

He had once a good, loving papa like

yours, when he was a tiny baby in long white clothes; but the dear papa marched away with the blue-coated soldiers one day, and never came back any more to his little children; for he died far, far away from home, on a green battlefield, with many other soldiers. You can think how sad and lonely Dicky's mamma was, and how she hugged her three babies close in her arms, and said:—

"Darlings, you have n't any father now, but the dear God will help your mother to take care of you!"

And now she was working hard, so very hard, from morning till night every day to get money to buy bread and milk and clothes for Bess and Dot and Dicky.

But Dicky was a good little fellow and helped his mamma ever so much, pulling out bastings from her needlework, bringing in the kindling and shavings from the shed, and going to the store for her butter and potatoes and eggs. So one morning she said:—

"Dicky, you have been such a help to me this summer, I'd like to give you something to make you very happy. Let us count the money in your bank — you earned it all yourself — and see what we could buy with it. To be sure, Bess wants a waterproof and Dot needs rubbers, but we do want our little boy to have a birthday present."

"Oh, mamma," cried he, clapping his hands, "what a happy day it will be! I shall buy that tool-box at the store round the corner! It's such a beauty, with a little saw, a claw-hammer, a chisel, a screw-driver, and everything a carpenter needs. It costs just a dollar, exactly!"

Then they unscrewed the bank and found ninety-five cents, so that it would take only five cents more to make the dollar. Dicky earned that before he went to bed, by piling up wood for a neighbor; and his mamma changed all the little five and ten cent pieces into two bright half-dollars that chinked together joyfully in his trousers pocket.

The next morning he was up almost at the same time the robins and chimney-swallows flew out of their nests; jumped down the stairs, two at a time, and could scarcely eat his breakfast, such a hurry as he was in to buy the precious tool-box. He opened the front door, danced down the wooden steps, and there on the curb in front of the house stood a little girl, with a torn gingham apron, no shoes, no hat, and her nut-brown curls flying in the wind; worse than all, she was crying as if her heart would break.

"Why, little girl, what's the matter?" asked Dicky, for he was a kind-hearted boy, and did n't like to see people cry.

She took down her apron and sobbed: —

"Oh, I've lost my darling little brown dog, and I can never get him back!"

"Why, has somebody poisoned him — is he dead?" said Dicky.

She shook her head.

"No, oh no! The pound-man took him away in his cart — my sweet little bit of a dog; he has such a cunning little curly tail, and long, silky ears; he does all kinds of tricks, and they'll never let me in at home without Bruno."

And then she began to cry harder than ever, so that Dicky hardly knew what to say to her.

Now the pound, children, is a very large place somewhere near the city, with a high fence all around it, and inside are kept colts and horses, the little calves and mother cows, and the sheep and goats that run away from home, or are picked up by the roadside The pound-man rides along the street in a big cart, which has a framework of slats built over it, so that it looks something like a chicken-coop on wheels, and in it — some of you have seen him do it — he puts the poor dogs that have n't collars on, and whose masters have n't paid for them. Then he rides away and locks them up in the great place inside the high fence, and they have to stay awhile. The dogs are killed if nobody comes for them.

"Well," said Dicky, "let us go and see the pound-man. Do you know where he lives?"

"Yes, indeed," answered the little girl, whose name was Lola. "I ran behind the cart all the way to the pound. I cried after Bruno, and Bruno whined for me, and poked his nose between the bars and tried to jump out, but he could n't. It's a pretty long way there, and the man is as cross as two sticks."

But they started off, and on and on they walked together, Dicky having tight hold of

Lola's hand, while she told him about the wonderful things Bruno could do; how he could go up and down a ladder, play the fife and beat the drum, make believe go to sleep, and dance a jig. It was by these tricks of his that Lola earned money for her uncle, with whom she lived; for her father and mother were both dead, and there was no one in the whole world who loved the little girl. The dear mother had died in a beautiful mountain country far across the ocean, and Lola and Bruno had been sent in a ship over to America. Now this dear, pretty mamma of Lola's used to sing to her when she rocked her to sleep, and as she grew from a baby to a tiny girl she learned the little songs to sing to Bruno when he was a little puppy. Would you like to hear one of them? She used to sing it on the street corners, and at the end of the last verse that knowing, cunning, darling Bruno would yawn as if he could not keep awake another minute, tuck his silky head between his two fore paws, shut his bright eyes, give a tired little sigh, and stay fast asleep until Lola waked him. This is the song:—

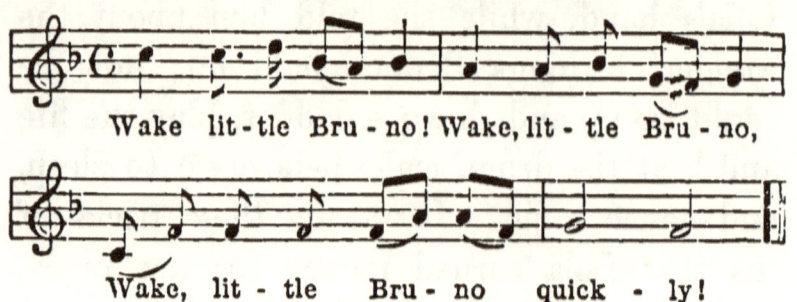

When the two children came to the pound and saw the little house at the gate where the pound-man lived, Dicky was rather frightened and hardly dared walk up the steps; but after a moment he thought to himself, "I won't be a coward; I have n't done anything wrong." So he gave the door a rousing knock, for an eight-year-old boy, and brought the man out at once.

"What do you want?" said he, in a gruff voice, for he did seem rather cross.

"Please, sir, I want Lola's little brown dog. He's all the dog she has, and she earns money with him. He does funny tricks for ten cents."

"How do you think I know whether I've got a brown dog in there or not?" growled he. "You'd better run home to your mothers, both of you."

At this Lola began to cry again, and Dicky said quickly: —

"Oh, you'd know him soon as anything, — he has such a cunning curly tail and long silky ears. His name is Bruno."

"Well," snapped the man, "where's your money? Hurry up! I want my breakfast."

"Money!" cried Dicky, looking at Lola.

"Money!" whispered little Lola, looking back at Dicky.

"Yes," said he, "of course! Give me a dollar and I will give you the dog."

"But," answered Lola, "I have n't a bit of money; I never have any."

"Neither have " — began Dicky; and then his fingers crept into his trousers pocket and felt the two silver half-dollars that were to buy his tool-box. He had forgotten all about that tool-box for an hour, but how could he — how could he ever give away that precious money which he had been so long in getting together, five cents at a time? He remembered the sharp little saw, the stout hammer, the cunning plane, bright chisel, and shining screw-driver, and his fingers closed round the money tightly; but just then he looked at pretty little Lola, with her sad face, her swollen eyes and the brave red lips she was trying to keep from quivering with tears. That was enough; he quickly drew out the silver dollar, and said to the pound-man: —

"Here's your dollar — give us the dog!"

The man looked much surprised. Not many little eight-year-old boys have a dollar in their trousers pocket.

"Where did you get it?" he asked.

"I earned every cent of it," answered poor Dicky with a lump in his throat and a choking voice. "I brought in coal and cut kindlings for most six months before I got enough, and there ain't another tool-box in the world so good as that one for a dollar — but I want Bruno!"

Then the pound-man showed them a little flight of steps that led up to a square hole in the wall of the pound, and told them to go up and look through it and see if the dog was there. They climbed up and put their two rosy eager faces at the rough little window. "Bruno! Bruno!" called little Lola, and no Bruno came; but every frightened homesick little doggy in that prison poked up

"'HERE'S YOUR DOLLAR—GIVE US THE DOG!'" (page 46)

his nose, wagged his tail, and started for the voice. It did n't matter whether they were Fidos, or Carlos, or Rovers, or Pontos; they knew that they were lonesome little dogs, and perhaps somebody had remembered them. Lola's tender heart ached at the sight of so many fatherless and motherless dogs, and she cried, —

"No, no, you poor darlings! I have n't come for you; I want my own Bruno."

"Sing for him, and may be he will come," said Dicky; and Lola leaned her elbow on the window sill and sang: —

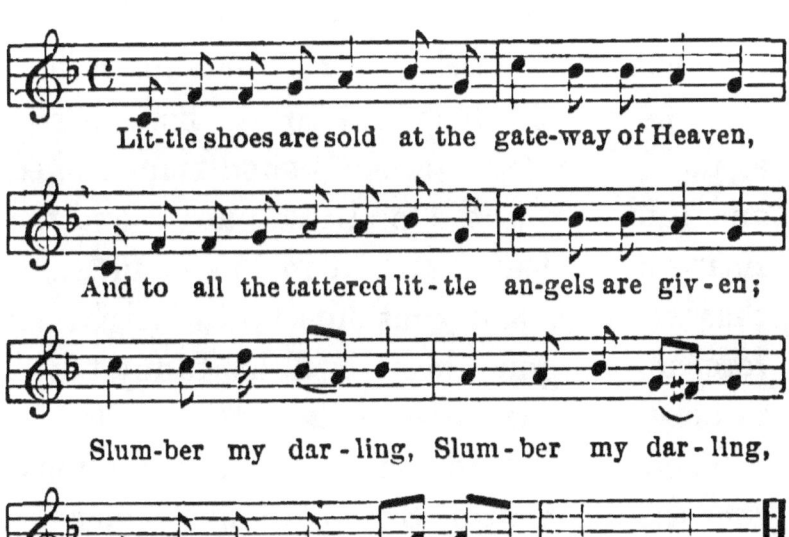

Lit-tle shoes are sold at the gate-way of Heaven,
And to all the tattered lit-tle an-gels are giv-en;
Slum-ber my dar-ling, Slum-ber my dar-ling,
Slum - ber my dar - ling sweet - ly.

Now Bruno was so tired with running from the pound-man, so hungry, so frightened, and so hoarse with barking that he had gone to sleep; but when he heard Lola's voice singing the song he knew so well, he started up, and out he bounded half awake — the dearest, loveliest little brown dog in the world, with a cunning curly tail sticking up in a round bob behind, two long silky ears that almost touched the ground, and four soft white feet.

Then they were two such glad children, and such a glad little brown dog was Bruno! Why, he kissed Lola's bare feet and hands and face, and nearly chewed her apron into rags, he was so delighted to see his mistress again. Even the cross pound-man smiled and said he was the prettiest puppy, and the smartest, he had ever had in the pound, and that when he had shut him up the night before he had gone through all his funny tricks in hopes that he would be let out.

Then Dicky and Lola walked back home over the dusty road, Bruno running along beside them, barking at the birds, sniffing at the squirrels, and chasing all the chickens and kittens he met on the way, till at last they reached the street corner, where Lola turned to go to her home, after kissing her new friend and thanking him for being so good and kind to her.

But what about Master Dicky himself, who had lost his tool-box? He did n't feel much like a smiling boy just then. He crept in at the back door, and when he saw his dear mother's face in the kitchen he could n't stand it a minute longer, but burst out crying, and told her all about it.

"Well, my little son," said she, "I 'm very, very sorry. I wish I could give you another dollar, but I have n't any money to spare. You did just right to help Lola find Bruno, and buy him back for her, and I 'm very proud of my boy; but you can't give away the dollar and have the tool-box too. So wipe your eyes, and try to be happy. You did n't eat any breakfast, dear, take a piece of nice bread and sugar."

So Dicky dried his tears and began to eat

After a while he wanted to wipe his sticky, sugary little mouth, and as he took his clean handkerchief out of his pocket, two shining, chinking, clinking round things tumbled out on the floor and rolled under the kitchen table! What could they have been! Why, his two silver half-dollars, to be sure. And where in the world did they come from, do you suppose? Why, it was the nicest, funniest thing! The pound-man was not so cross after all, for he thought Lola and Dicky were two such kind children, and Bruno such a cunning dog, that he could not bear to take Dicky's dollar away from him; so while the little boy was looking the other way the pound-man just slipped the money back into Dick's bit of a pocket without saying a word. Was n't that a beautiful surprise?

So Dicky ran to the corner store as fast as his feet could carry him, and bought the toolbox.

Every Saturday afternoon he has such a pleasant time playing with it! And who do you suppose sits on the white kitchen floor with Dot and Bess, watching him make dolls' tables and chairs with his carpenter's tools? Why, Lola, to be sure, and a little brown dog too, with a cunning curly tail turned up in a round bob behind, and two long silky ears touching the floor. For Dick's mamma had such a big heart that I do believe it would have held all the children in the world, and as Lola's uncle didn't care for her the least little bit, he gave her to this mamma of Dicky's, who grew to love this little girl almost as well as she loved her own Dicky and Dot and Bess.

AQUA; OR, THE WATER BABY.[1]

"This standing above life, and yet grasping life, and being stirred by life, is what makes the genuine educator." — FROEBEL.

It was a clear, sunshiny day, and out on the great, wide, open sea there sparkled thousands and thousands of water-drops. One of these was a merry little fellow who danced on the silver backs of the fishes as they plunged up and down in the waves, and, no matter how high he sprung, always came down again plump into his mother's lap.

His mother, you know, was the Ocean, and very beautiful she looked that summer day in her dark blue dress and white ruffles.

By and by the happy water-drop tired of

---

[1] The plan of this story was suggested to me many years ago; so many, indeed, that I cannot now remember whether it was my friend's own, or whether he had read something like it in German. — K. D. W.

his play, and looking up to the clear sky above him thought he would like to have a sail on one of the white floating clouds; so, giving a jump from the Ocean's arms, he begged the Sun to catch him up and let him go on a journey to see the earth.

The Sun said "Yes," and took ever so many other drops too, so that Aqua might not be lonesome on the way. He did not know this, however, for they all had been changed into fine mist or vapor. Do you know what vapor is? If you breathe into the air, when it is cold enough, you will see it coming out of your mouth like steam, and you may also see very hot steam coming from the nose of a kettle of boiling water. When it is quite near to the earth, where we can see it, we call it "fog." The water-drops had been changed into vapor because in their own shape they were too heavy for sunbeams to carry.

Higher and higher they sailed, so fast that they grew quite dizzy; why, in an hour they had gone over a hundred miles! and how grand it was, to be looking down on the world below, and sailing faster than fish can swim or birds can fly!

But after a while it grew nearly time for the Sun to go to bed; he became very red in the face, and began to sink lower and lower, until suddenly he went clear out of sight!

Poor little Aqua could not help being frightened, for every minute it grew darker and colder. At last he thought he would try to get back to the earth again, so he slipped away, and as he fell lower and lower he grew heavier, until he was a little round, bright drop again, and alighted on a rosebush. A lovely velvet bud opened its leaves, and in he slipped among the crimson cushions, to sleep until morning. Then the leaves opened, and rolling over in his bed he called out, "Please, dear Sun, take me with you again." So the sunbeams caught him up a second time, and they flew through the air till the noon-time, when it grew warmer and warmer, and there was no red rose to hide him, not even a blade of grass to shade his tired head; but just as he was crying out, "Please, King Sun, let me go back to the dear mother Ocean," the wind took pity on him, and came with its cool breath and fanned him, with all his brothers, into a heavy gray cloud, after which he blew them apart and told them to join hands and hurry away to the earth. Helter-skelter down they went, rolling over each other pell-mell, till with a patter and clatter and spatter they touched the ground, and all the people cried, "It rains."

Some of the drops fell on a mountain side, Aqua among them, and down the rocky cliff he ran, leading the way for his brothers. Soon, together they plunged into a mountain brook, which came foaming and dashing along, leaping over rocks and rushing down the hillside, till in the valley below they heard the strangest clattering noise.

On the bank stood a flour-mill, and at the door a man whose hat and clothes were gray with dust.

Inside the mill were two great stones, which kept whizzing round and round, faster than a boy's top could spin, worked by the big wheel outside; and these stones ground the wheat into flour and the corn into golden meal.

But what giant do you suppose it was who could turn and swing that tremendous wheel, together with those heavy stones? No giant at all. No one but our tiny little water-drops themselves, who sprang on it by hundreds and thousands, and whirled it over and over.

The brook emptied into a quiet pond where ducks and geese were swimming. Such a still, beautiful place it was, with the fuzzy, brown cat-tails lifting their heads above the water, and the yellow cow lilies, with their leaves like green platters, floating on the top. On the edge lived the fat green bullfrogs, and in the water were spotted trout, silver shiners, cunning minnows, and other fish.

Aqua liked this place so much that he stayed a good while, sailing up and down, taking the ducks' backs for ships and the frogs for horses; but after a time he tired of the dull life, and he and his brothers floated out over a waterfall and under a bridge for a long, long distance, until they saw another brook tumbling down a hillside.

"Come, let's join hands!" cried Aqua; and so they all dashed on together till they came to a broad river which opened its arms to them.

By the help of Aqua and his brothers the beautiful river was able to float heavy ships, though not so long ago it was only a little rill, through which a child could wade or over which he could step. Here a vessel loaded with lumber was carried just as easily as if it had been a paper boat; there a steamer, piled with boxes and barrels, and crowded with people, passed by, its great wheel crashing through the water and leaving a long trail, as of foamy soapsuds, behind it. On and ever on the river went, seeking the ocean, and whether it hurried round a corner or glided smoothly on its way to the sea, there was always something new and strange to be seen — busy cities, quiet little towns, buzzing sawmills, stone bridges, and harbors full of all sorts of vessels, large and small, with flags of all colors floating from the masts and sailors of all countries working on the decks. But Aqua did not stay long in any place, for as the river grew wider and wider, and nearer and nearer its end, he could almost see the mother Ocean into whose arms he was joyfully running. She reached out to gather all her children, the water-drops, into her heart, and closer than all the others nestled our little Aqua.

His travels were over, his pleasures and dangers past; and he was folded again to the dear mother heart, the safest, sweetest place in all the whole wide world. In warm, still summer evenings, if you will take a walk on the sea-beach, you will hear the gentle rippling swash of the waves; and some very wise people think it must be the gurgling voices of Aqua and his brother water-drops telling each other about their wonderful journey round the world.

MOUFFLOU.

ADAPTED FROM OUIDA.

"We tell too few stories to children, and those we tell are stories whose heroes are automata and stuffed dolls."
— FROEBEL.

Lolo and Moufflou lived far away from here, in a sunny country called Italy.

Lolo was not as strong as you are, and could never run about and play, for he was lame, poor fellow, and always had to hop along on a little crutch. He was never well enough to go to school, but as his fingers were active and quick he could plait straw matting and make baskets at home. He had four or five rosy, bright little brothers and sisters, but they were all so strong and could play all day so easily that Lolo was not with them much; so Moufflou was his very best friend, and they were together all day long.

Moufflou was a snow-white poodle, with

such soft, curly wool that he looked just like a lamb; and the man who gave him to the children, when he was a little puppy, had called him "Moufflon," which meant sheep in his country.

Lolo's father had died four years before; but he had a mother, who had to work very hard to keep the children clean and get them enough to eat. He had, too, a big brother Tasso, who worked for a gardener, and every Saturday night brought his wages home to help feed and clothe the little children. Tasso was almost a man now, and in that country as soon as you grow to be a man you have to go away and be a soldier; so Lolo's mother was troubled all the time for fear that her Tasso would be taken away. If you have money enough, you can always pay some one to go in your place; but Tasso had no money, and neither had the poor mother, so every day she was anxious lest her boy might have to go to the wars.

But Lolo and Moufflou knew nothing of all this, and every day, when Lolo was well enough, they were happy together. They would walk up the streets, or sit on the church steps, or, if the day was fair, would perhaps go into the country and bring home great bundles of yellow and blue and crimson flowers.

The tumble-down old house in which the family lived was near a tall, gray church. It was a beautiful old church, and all the children loved it, but Lolo most of all. He loved it in the morning, when the people brought in great bunches of white lilies to trim it; and at noon, when it was cool and shady; and at sunset, when the long rays shone through the painted windows and made blue and golden and violet lights on the floor.

One morning Lolo and Moufflou were sitting on the church steps and watching the people, when a gentleman who was passing by stopped to look at the dog.

"That's a very fine poodle," he said.

"Indeed he is," cried Lolo. "But you should see him on Sundays when he is just washed; then he is as white as snow."

"Can he do any tricks?" asked the gentleman.

"I should say so," said Lolo, for he had taught the dog all he knew. "He can stand on his hind legs, he can dance, he can speak, he can make a wheelbarrow of himself, and when I put a biscuit on his nose and count one, two, three, he will snap and catch the biscuit."

The gentleman said he should like to see some of the tricks, and Moufflou was very glad to do them, for no one had ever whipped him or hurt him, and he loved to do what his little master wished. Then the gentleman told Lolo that he had a little boy at home, so weak and so sick that he could not get up from the sofa, and that he would like to have Lolo bring the poodle to show him the next day, so he gave Lolo some money, and told him the name of the hotel where he was staying.

Lolo went hopping home as fast as his little crutch could carry him, and went quickly upstairs to his mother.

"Oh, mamma!" he said. "See the money a gentleman gave me, and all because dear Moufflou did his pretty tricks so nicely. Now you can have your coffee every morning, and Tasso can have his new suit for Sunday." Then he told his mother about the gentleman,

"'HE WILL SNAP AND CATCH THE BISCUIT'" (page 62)

and that he had promised to take Moufflou to see him the next day.

So when the morning came, Moufflou was washed as white as snow, and his pretty curls were tied up with blue ribbon, and they both trotted off. Moufflou was so proud of his curls and his ribbon that he hardly liked to put his feet on the ground at all. They were shown to the little boy's room, where he lay on the sofa very pale and unhappy. A bright little look came into his eyes when he saw the dog, and he laughed when Moufflou did his tricks. How he clapped his hands when he saw him make a wheelbarrow, and he tossed them both handfuls of cakes and candies! Neither the boy nor the dog ever had quite enough to eat, so they nibbled the little cakes with their sharp, white teeth, and were very glad.

When Lolo got up to go, the little boy began to cry, and said, "Oh, I want the dog. Let me have the dog!"

"Oh, indeed I can't," said Lolo, "he is my own Moufflou, and I cannot let you have him."

The little boy was so unhappy and cried so

bitterly that Lolo was very sorry to see him, and he went quickly down the stairs with Moufflou. The gentleman gave him more money this time, and he was so excited and so glad that he went very fast all the way home, swinging himself over the stones on his little crutch. But when he opened the door, there was his mother crying as if her heart would break, and all the children were crying in a corner, and even Tasso was home from his work, looking very unhappy.

"Oh! what *is* the matter?" cried Lolo. But no one answered him, and Moufflou, seeing them all so sad, sat down and threw up his nose in the air and howled a long, sad howl. By and by one of the children told Lolo that at last Tasso had been chosen to be a soldier, and that he must soon go away to the war. The poor mother said, crying, that she did not know what would become of her little children through the long, cold winter.

Lolo showed her his money, but she was too unhappy even to care for that, and so by and by he went to his bed with Moufflou. The dog had always slept at Lolo's feet, but this night he crept close up by the side of his little master, and licked his hand now and then to show that he was sorry.

The next morning Lolo and Moufflou went with Tasso to the gardens where he worked, and all the way along the bright river and among the green trees they talked together of what they should do when Tasso had gone. Tasso said that if they could only get some money he would not have to go away to the wars, but he shook his head sadly and knew that no one would lend it to them. At noon Lolo went home with Moufflou to his dinner. When they had finished (it was only bean soup and soon eaten), the mother told Lolo that his aunt wanted him to go and see her that afternoon, and take care of the children while she went out. So Lolo put on his hat, called Moufflou, and was limping toward the door, when his mother said: —

"No, don't take the dog to-day, your aunt does n't like him; leave him here with me."

"Leave Moufflou?" said Lolo, "why, I never leave him; he would n't know what to do without me all the afternoon."

"Yes, leave him," said his mother. "I

don't want you to take him with you. Don't let me tell you again." So Lolo turned around and went down the stairs, feeling very sad at leaving his dear Moufflou even for a short time. But the hours went by, and when night-time came he hurried back to the little old home. He stood at the bottom of the long, dark stairway and called "Moufflou! Moufflou!" but no doggie came; then he climbed half-way up to the landing and called again, "Moufflou!" but no little white feet came pattering down. Up to the top of the stairs went poor tired Lolo and opened the door.

"Why, where is my Moufflou?" he said.

The mother had been crying, and she looked very sad and did not answer him for a moment.

"Where is my Moufflou?" asked Lolo again, "what have you done with my dear Moufflou?"

"He is sold," the mother said at last, "sold to the gentleman who has the little lame boy. He came here to-day, and he likes the dog so much and his little boy was so pleased at the pretty tricks he does, that he told me he would give a great deal of money if I would sell him the dog. Just think, Lolo, he gave me so much money that we can pay somebody now to go to the war for Tasso."

But before she had finished talking, Lolo began to grow white and cold and to waver to and fro, so that his little crutch could hardly support him. When she had done he called out, "My Moufflou — my Moufflou sold!" and he threw his hands up over his head and fell all in a heap on the floor, his poor little crutch clattering down beside him. His mother took him up and laid him on his bed, but all night long he tossed to and fro, calling for his dog. When the morning came, his little hands and his head were very, very hot, and by and by the doctor came and said he had a fever. He asked the mother what it was the little boy was calling for, and she told him that it was his dog, and that he had been sold. The doctor shook his head, and then went away.

Day after day poor Lolo lay on his bed. His hair had been cut short, he did not know his brothers and sisters, nor his mother, and his little aching head went to and fro, to and fro, on the pillow from morning till night. Once Tasso went to the hotel to find the gentleman. He was going to tell him to take the money and give him back the dog; but the gentleman had gone many miles away on the cars and taken Moufflou with him. So every day Lolo grew weaker, until the doctor said that he must die very soon.

One afternoon they were all in the room with him. The windows were wide open. His mother sat by his bed and the children on the floor beside her; even Tasso was at home helping to take care of his little brother. All was so still that you could hear poor Lolo's faint breath, when — suddenly — there was a scampering and a pattering of little feet on the stairs, and a white poodle dashed into the room and jumped on the bed. It was Moufflou! but you would never have known him, for he was so thin that you could count all his bones. His curls were dirty and matted, and full of sticks and straws and burrs; his feet were dusty and bleeding, and you could tell in a moment that he had traveled a great many miles. When he jumped on the bed, Lolo opened his eyes a little. He saw it was Moufflou, and laid one little thin hand on the dog's head; then he turned on his pillow, closed his eyes, and went quietly to sleep. Moufflou would not get off the bed, and would eat nothing unless they brought it to him there. He only lay close by his little master, with his brown eyes wide open, looking straight into his face. By and by the doctor came, and said that Lolo was really a little better, and that perhaps he might get well now. The mother and Tasso were very glad indeed, but they knew that the gentleman would come back for his dog, and they scarcely knew what to do, nor what to say to him. Lolo grew a little stronger every day, and at the end of a week a man came upstairs asking if Moufflou was there. They had taken him a long way off, but he had run away from them one day, and they had never been able to find him. Tasso asked the messenger to let Moufflou stay until he had seen the gentleman, and he took the money and put on his hat and went with him to the hotel. The sick boy was in the room with his father, and Tasso went straight to them and told them all about it: that Lolo nearly died without his dear Moufflou, that day after day he lay in his bed calling for the dog, and that at last one afternoon Moufflou came back to them, thin and hungry and dirty, but so glad to see his little master again. Nobody knew, said Tasso, how he could have found his way so many miles alone, but there he was, and now he begged the gentleman to be so kind as to take back the money. He would go and be a soldier, if he must; but Lolo and his dog must never be parted again.

The gentleman told Tasso that he seemed to be a kind brother, and that he might keep the money and the dog too, if only he would find them another poodle and teach him to be as wise and faithful as Moufflou was. Tasso was so glad that he thanked them again and again, and hurried home to tell Lolo and his mother the good news. He soon found a poodle almost as pretty as Moufflou, and every day Lolo, who has grown strong now, helps Tasso to teach him all of Moufflou's tricks.

Sometimes Lolo turns and puts his arms around Moufflou's neck and says, —

"Tell me, my Moufflou, how you ever came back to me, over all the rivers, and all the bridges, and all the miles of road?"

Moufflou can never answer him, but I think he must have found his way home because he loved his master so much; and the grown people always say, "Love will find out the way."

BENJY IN BEASTLAND.

ADAPTED FROM MRS. EWING.

"With the genuine story-teller the inner life of the genuine listener is roused; he is carried out of himself, and he thereby measures himself." — FROEBEL.

BENJY was a very naughty, disagreeable boy! It is sad to say it, but it is truth. He always had a cloudy, smudgy, slovenly look, like a slate half-washed, that made one feel how nice it would be if he could be scrubbed inside and out with hot water and soap.

Benjy was the only boy in the family, but he had two little sisters who were younger than he. They were dear, merry little things, and many boys would have found them pleasant little playmates; but Benjy had shown how much he disliked to play with them, and it made them feel very badly. One of them said one day, "Benjy does not care for us because we are only girls, so we have taken Nox for our brother." Nox was a big curly dog, something like a Newfoundland.

Now Benjy was not at all handsome, and he hated tubs and brushes and soap and water. He liked to lie abed late in the mornings, and when he got up he had only time enough to half wash himself. But Nox rose early, liked cold water, had snow-white teeth and glossy hair, and when you spoke to him he looked straight up at you with his clear honest brown eyes. Benjy's jacket and shirt-front were always spotted with dirt, while the covering of Nox's chest was glossy and well kept. Benjy came into the parlor with muddy boots and dirty hands; but Nox, if he had been out in the mud, would lie down when he came home, and lick his brown paws till they were quite clean. Benjy liked to kill all kinds of animals, but Nox saved lives, though he often came near losing his own.

Near their home was a deep river, where many a dog and cat was drowned. There was one place on the bank of this river where there was an old willow-tree, which spread its branches wide and stretched its long arms till they touched the water. Here Nox used to bring everything that he found in the river.

I must tell you that Benjy did not like Nox, and with very good reason. Benjy had had something to do with the death of several animals belonging to the people in the neighborhood, and he had tied stones or tin cans around their necks and dropped them into the river. But Nox used to wander round quite early in the morning, and very often found in the river and brought out what Benjy had thrown in, and this is why he did not like the brave dog.

There was another dog in the family, named Mr. Rough. His eyes had been almost scratched out by cats, his little body bore marks of many beatings, and he had a hoarse bark which sounded as if he had a bad cold.

If Benjy cared for any animal, it was for Mr. Rough, although he treated him worse than he did Nox, because he was small.

One day Benjy felt very mischievous; he even played a cruel trick on Nox while he was asleep. As he sat near to him he kept lightly pricking the dog's lips with a fine needle. The dog would half wake up, shake his head, rub his lips with his paws, and then drop off to sleep again.

At last this cruel boy stuck the needle in too far and hurt poor Nox, who jumped up with a start, and as he did so the needle broke off, part of it staying in the flesh, where, after a great deal of work which hurt the poor dog dreadfully, the little sisters found it. How they cried for their pet! The braver one held Nox's lips and pulled out the needle, while the other wiped the tears from her sister's eyes, that she might see what she was doing. Nox sat still and moaned and wagged his tail very feebly, but when it was over he fairly knocked the little sisters down in his eagerness to show his gratitude. But Benjy went out and found Mr. Rough, and as he did not feel like being kind to any one, he kicked him, and Mr. Rough for the first time ran away. Benjy could not find him, but he found a boy as naughty as himself, who was chasing another little dog and pelting it with stones. This would have been very good fun, but one of the stones struck the dog and killed him. So the boys tied something around his neck and threw him into the river.

Benjy went to bed early that night, but he could not sleep, because he was thinking of that little white dog, and wishing he had not thrown him into the river; so at last he got up and went to the willow-tree. He looked up through the branches and saw the moon shining down at him, and it seemed so large and so close that he thought if he were only on the highest part of the tree he could touch it with his hand. While he was looking he thought of a book his mother had, which told him that all animals went up into the moon after they left the earth.

"I wonder," said Benjy, "if that dog we killed last night is really up there."

The Man in the Moon looked down on him just then, and, to his surprise, said: —

"This is Beastland. Won't you come up and see if the dog is here? Can you climb?"

"I guess I can," said Benjy, and he climbed up first on one branch, then up higher on to another, till he stood on the very top, and all he could see about him was a shining white light.

"Walk right in," said the Man in the Moon. "Put out your feet, — don't be afraid!" So

Benjy stepped into the moon and found himself in Beastland.

Oh! it was such a funny place, and yet it was very beautiful. There were many more beasts there than in a menagerie, and they were so polite to each other, too, and so merry and kind to Benjy, that it made him feel quite at home.

A nice old spider was anxious to teach him how to make a web. So he said to Benjy:—

"When you are ready, look around and find a spot where you can tie your first line; then you have a ball of thread inside of you, of course."

"I can't say that I have," said Benjy, "but I have a good deal of string in my pocket."

"Oh, well!" said the spider, "that is all right; whether it's in your pocket or your stomach it is all the same."

Just as the spider was giving Benjy his lesson, one animal whispered to another, and that one to another, who and what Benjy was. Dear me! in a minute the beasts all changed their way of treating him. They called him *Boy!* and up there that meant something not at all nice. Then they took him to the Lion, the king of all the beasts, and asked him what should be done with the Boy.

The Lion said: "If you want me to have anything to do with this trouble, you must mind me. First, however, we will hear what Benjy has to say for himself."

They all placed themselves in a circle, the Lion on a high chair, (because, you know, he was going to be judge, and all judges sit in big chairs,) and Benjy sat in the middle of the circle.

"Now, what has the Boy done?" asked the Lion.

"He stones and drowns dogs, and he hurts and kills cats," shouted the beasts all together.

"Mr. Rough kills the cats," said Benjy, because he was frightened.

"Very well," said the Lion, "we will send some one down for Mr. Rough."

So they all waited, and in a little while they heard the jingling of Mr. Rough's collar, and he walked into the circle with his little short tail standing right up.

"Mr. Rough," said the Lion, "Benjy says it is you, and not he, who tease and kill the cats."

"Well," said Mr. Rough, jumping about in an angry way, "am I to blame? *Bouf, bouf,* who taught me to do it? *Bouf, bouf,* it was that Boy over there. *Bouf-bouf!*"

Then Mr. Rough told them that Benjy had made him tease and worry the cats and dogs so often that he had quite learned to like it. All the beasts were very angry at this, and said that Benjy must be punished.

The Lion said that he did not know just then what was best to be done with Benjy, so he asked the beasts if they would wait till he had walked around and thought about it. They said yes, so he walked around the circle seven times, lashing his tail in the grandest way; then he took his seat again and said:—

"Gentle beasts, birds and fishes, you have all heard what this Boy has done, and you would like him to be treated as he has treated you. We will not abuse Benjy, but I do not think he is good enough to stay with us. We will tie a tin-kettle to him and chase him from Beastland, and Mr. Rough shall be our leader."

This was no sooner said than done. The Lion gave one dreadful roar as a signal for the animals to begin the chase.

With the tin-kettle fastened to him and hurting him at every step, and with Mr. Rough at his very heels, Benjy was run out of Beastland. When he got to the edge of the moon he jumped off, Mr. Rough after him.

Down, down, they went, oh! so fast and so far! Benjy screaming all the way and Mr. Rough's collar jingling. They came to the river, and making all the noise they could, in they fell. As Benjy sank he thought of all the unkind things he had done. He came to the top, but sank again, and sinking, thought of his papa and mamma and his little sisters, and of his nice little bed, and of the prayers his dear mamma used to hear him say. He rose for the last time, and saw Nox standing on the bank, and thought, "Now he has come to do something to me because I have so often hurt him." Down, down he went, as a lark flew up in the summer sky. The bird was almost out of sight when a soft black nose and great brown eyes came close to his face, and a kind, gentle mouth took hold of him, and paddling and swimming as hard as he could, Nox carried Benjy to the shore and laid him under the willow-tree. There Benjy's papa found him, and took him home, where he was sick for a long, long time. When he got a little better he used to tell people of his visit to Beastland, but they always said it was only a dream he had during the fever.

In the long weeks of his sickness he grew much kinder and sweeter. But something happened when he was getting well which softened his little heart once and forever.

While he was sick, Mr. Rough was given to one of the servants to be cared for and fed well, but he did not treat him kindly, and besides, the dog wanted his little master; he wanted to see him, but no one would let him; so poor faithful Mr. Rough got thinner and weaker every day, till at last he would not eat anything nor even go out for a little walk.

One day the barn door was open and Mr. Rough thought of Benjy and crept into the house. When he got into the front hall he smelled Benjy and ran into the parlor; and when he got into the parlor he saw Benjy, who had heard the jingle of his collar and who stood up and held out his arms for him. Mr. Rough jumped into them, and then fell dead at his master's feet.

Yes, dear children, Mr. Rough died of joy at seeing Benjy again. Benjy felt very sorry for him, and it kept him from growing well for a long time, but it did him good in other ways, for as the tears rolled down his cheeks on to Mr. Rough's poor little scratched face, he felt as if he never could hurt or be unkind to any animal again.

THE PORCELAIN STOVE.

ADAPTED FROM OUIDA.

"The story-teller must take life into himself in its wholeness, must let it live and work whole and free within him. He must give it out free and unabbreviated, and yet *stand above the life* which actually is." — FROEBEL.

IN a little brown house, far, far away in Germany, there lived a father and his children. There were ever so many of them, — let me see, — Hilda, the dear eldest sister, and Hans, the big, strong brother; then Karl and August, and the baby Marta. Just enough for the fingers of one hand. How many is that? But it is Karl that I am going to tell you about. He was nine years old, a rosy little fellow, with big bright eyes and a curly head as brown as a ripe nut. The dear mother was dead, and the father was very poor, so that Karl and his brothers and sisters sometimes knew what it was to be hungry; but they were happy, for they loved each other very dearly, and ate their brown bread and milk without wishing it were something nicer. One afternoon Karl had been sent on a long journey. It was winter time, and he had to run fast over the frozen fields of white snow. The night was coming on, and he was hurrying home with a great jug of milk, feeling cold and tired. The mountains looked high and white and still in the cold moonlight, and the stars seemed to say, when they twinkled, "Hurry, Karl! the children are hungry." At last he saw a little brown cottage, with a snow-laden roof and a shining window, through which he could see the bright firelight dancing merrily, — for Hilda never closed the shutters till all the boys were safely inside the house. When he saw the dear home-light he ran as fast as his feet could carry him, burst in at the low front door, kissed Hilda, and shouted:—

"Oh! dear, dear Hirschvogel! I am so glad to get back to you again; you are every bit as good as the summer time."

Now, Hirschvogel was not one of the family, as you might think, nor even a splendid dog, nor a pony, but it was a large, beautiful porcelain stove, so tall that it quite touched the ceiling. It stood at the end of the room, shining with all the hues of a peacock's tail, bright and warm and beautiful; its great golden feet were shaped like the claws of a lion, and there was a golden crown on the very top of all. You never have seen a stove like it, for it was white where our stoves are black, and it had flowers and birds and beautiful ladies and grand gentlemen painted all over it, and everywhere it was brilliant with gold and bright colors. It was a very old stove, for sixty years before, Karl's grandfather had dug it up out of some broken-down buildings where he was working, and, finding it strong and whole, had taken it home; and ever since then it had stood in the big room, warming the children, who tumbled like little flowers around its shining feet. The grandfather did not know it, but it was a wonderful stove, for it had been made by a great potter named Hirschvogel.

A potter, you know, children, is a man who makes all sorts of things, dishes and tiles and vases, out of china and porcelain and clay. So the family had always called the stove

Hirschvogel, after the potter, just as if it were alive.

To the children the stove was very dear indeed. In summer they laid a mat of fresh moss all around it, and dressed it up with green boughs and beautiful wild flowers. In winter, scampering home from school over the ice and snow, they were always happy, knowing that they would soon be cracking nuts or roasting chestnuts in the heat and light of the dear old stove. All the children loved it, but Karl even more than the rest, and he used to say to himself, "When I grow up I will make just such things too, and then I will set Hirschvogel up in a beautiful room that I will build myself. That's what I will do when I'm a man."

After Karl had eaten his supper, this cold night, he lay down on the floor by the stove, the children all around him, on the big wolfskin rug. With some sticks of charcoal he was drawing pictures for them of what he had seen all day. When the children had looked enough at one picture, he would sweep it out with his elbow and make another — faces, and dogs' heads, and men on sleds, and old women in their furs, and pine-trees, and all sorts of animals. When they had been playing in this way for some time, Hilda, the eldest sister, said: —

"It is time for you all to go to bed, children. Father is very late to-night; you must not sit up for him."

"Oh, just five minutes more, dear Hilda," they begged. "Hirschvogel is so warm; the beds are never so warm as he is."

In the midst of their chatter and laughter the door opened, and in blew the cold wind and snow from outside. Their father had come home. He seemed very tired, and came slowly to his chair. At last he said, "Take the children to bed, daughter."

Karl stayed, curled up before the stove. When Hilda came back, the father said sadly:

"Hilda, I have sold Hirschvogel! I have sold it to a traveling peddler, for I need money very much; the winter is so cold and the children are so hungry. The man will take it away to-morrow."

Hilda gave a cry. "Oh, father! the children, in the middle of winter!" and she turned as white as the snow outside.

Karl lay half blind with sleep, staring at his father. "It can't be true, it can't be true!" he cried. "You are making fun, father." It seemed to him that the skies must fall if Hirschvogel were taken away.

"Yes," said the father, "you will find it true enough. The peddler has paid half the money to-night, and will pay me the other half to-morrow when he packs up the stove and takes it away."

"Oh, father! dear father!" cried poor little Karl, "you cannot mean what you say. Send our stove away? We shall all die in the dark and cold. Listen! I will go and try to get work to-morrow. I will ask them to let me cut ice or make the paths through the snow. There must be something I can do, and I will beg the people we owe money to, to wait. They are all neighbors; they will be patient. But sell Hirschvogel! Oh, never, never, never! Give the money back to the man."

The father was so sorry for his little boy that he could not speak. He looked sadly at him; then took the lamp that stood on the table, and left the room.

Hilda knelt down and tried to comfort

Karl, but he was too unhappy to listen. "I shall stay here," was all he said, and he lay there all the night long. The lamp went out; the rats came and ran across the room; the room grew colder and colder. Karl did not move, but lay with his face down on the floor by the lovely rainbow-colored stove. When it grew light, his sister came down with a lamp in her hand to begin her morning work. She crept up to him, and laid her cheek on his softly, and said:—

"Dear Karl, you must be frozen. Karl! do look up; do speak."

"Ah!" said poor Karl, "it will never be warm again."

Soon after some one knocked at the door. A strange voice called through the keyhole,—

"Let me in! quick! there is no time to lose. More snow like this and the roads will all be blocked. Let me in! Do you hear? I am come to take the great stove."

Hilda unfastened the door. The man came in at once, and began to wrap the stove in a great many wrappings, and carried it out into the snow, where an ox-cart stood in waiting. In another moment it was gone; gone forever!

Karl leaned against the wall, his tears falling like rain down his pale cheeks.

An old neighbor came by just then, and, seeing the boy, said to him: "Child, is it true your father is selling that big painted stove?"

Karl nodded his head, and began to sob again. "I love it! I love it!" he said.

"Well, if I were you I would do better than cry. I would go after it when I grew bigger," said the neighbor, trying to cheer him up a little. "Don't cry so loud; you will see your stove again some day," and the old man went away, leaving a new idea in Karl's head.

"Go after it," the old man had said. Karl thought, "Why not go with it?" He loved it better than anything else in the world, even better than Hilda. He ran off quickly after the cart which was carrying the dear Hirschvogel to the station. How he managed it he never knew very well himself, but it was certain that when the freight train moved away from the station Karl was hidden behind the stove. It was very dark, but he wasn't frightened. He was close beside Hirschvogel, but he wanted to be closer still; he meant to get inside the stove. He set to work like a little mouse to make a hole in the straw and hay. He gnawed and nibbled, and pushed and pulled, making a hole where he guessed that the door might be. At last he found it; he slipped through it, as he had so often done at home for fun, and curled himself up. He drew the hay and straw together carefully, and fixed the ropes, so that no one could have dreamed that a little mouse had been at them. Safe inside his dear Hirschvogel, he went as fast asleep as if he were in his own little bed at home. The train rumbled on in its heavy, slow way, and Karl slept soundly for a long time. When he awoke the darkness frightened him, but he felt the cold sides of Hirschvogel, and said softly, "Take care of me, dear Hirschvogel, oh, please take care of me!"

Every time the train stopped, and he heard the banging, stamping, and shouting, his heart seemed to jump up into his mouth. When the people came to lift the stove out, would they find him? and if they did find him, would they kill him? The thought, too, of Hilda, kept tugging at his heart now and then, but he said to himself, "If I can take Hirschvogel back to her, how pleased she will be, and how she will clap her hands!" He was not at all selfish in his love for Hirschvogel; he wanted it for them at home quite as much as for himself. That was what he kept thinking of all the way in the darkness and stillness which lasted so long. At last the train stopped, and awoke him from a half sleep. Karl felt the stove lifted by some men, who carried it to a cart, and then they started again on the journey, up hill and down, for what seemed miles and miles. Where they were going Karl had no idea. Finally the cart stopped; then it seemed as though they were carrying the stove up some stairs. The men rested sometimes, and then moved on again, and their feet went so softly he thought they must be walking on thick carpets. By and by the stove was set down again, happily for Karl, for he felt as though he should scream, or do something to make known that he was there. Then the wrappings were taken off, and he heard a voice say, "What a beautiful, beautiful stove!"

Next some one turned the round handle of

"'OH, LET ME STAY, PLEASE LET ME STAY'" (page 93)

the brass door, and poor little Karl's heart stood still.

"What is this?" said the man. "A live child!"

Then Karl sprang out of the stove and fell at the feet of the man who had spoken.

"Oh, let me stay, please let me stay!" he said. "I have come all the way with my darling Hirschvogel!"

The man answered kindly, "Poor little child! tell me how you came to hide in the stove. Do not be afraid. I am the king."

Karl was too much in earnest to be afraid; he was so glad, so glad it was the king, for kings must be always kind, he thought.

"Oh, dear king!" he said with a trembling voice, "Hirschvogel was ours, and we have loved it all our lives, and father sold it, and when I saw that it really did go from us I said to myself that I would go with it; and I do beg you to let me live with it, and I will go out every morning and cut wood for it and for all your other stoves, if only you will let me stay beside it. No one has ever fed it with wood but me since I grew big enough, and it loves me; it does indeed!" And then he lifted up his little pale face to the young king, who saw that great tears were running down his cheeks.

"Can't I stay with Hirschvogel?" he pleaded.

"Wait a little," said the king. "What do you want to be when you are a man? Do you want to be a wood-chopper?"

"I want to be a painter," cried Karl. "I want to be what Hirschvogel was. I mean the potter that made my Hirschvogel."

"I understand," answered the king, and he looked down at the child, and smiled. "Get up, my little man," he said in a kind voice; "I will let you stay with your Hirschvogel. You shall stay here, and you shall be taught to be a painter, but you must grow up very good, and when you are twenty-one years old, if you have done well, then I will give you back your beautiful stove." Then he smiled again and stretched out his hand. Karl threw his two arms about the king's knees and kissed his feet, and then all at once he was so tired and so glad and hungry and happy, that he fainted quite away on the floor.

Then the king had a letter written to Karl's

father, telling him that Karl had drawn him some beautiful charcoal pictures, and that he liked them so much he was going to take care of him until he was old enough to paint wonderful stoves like Hirschvogel. And he did take care of him for a long time, and when Karl grew older, he often went for a few days to his old home, where his father still lives.

In the little brown house stands Hirschvogel, tall and splendid, with its peacock colors as beautiful as ever, — the king's present to Hilda; and Karl never goes home without going into the great church and giving his thanks to God, who blessed his strange winter's journey in the great porcelain stove.

THE BABES IN THE WOOD.

"Nature and life speak very early to man." — FROEBEL.

A GREAT many years ago three little girls lived in an old-fashioned house in the East. They had a very lovely home, and a kind father and mother, who tried to make them happy. All through the summer they used to roam over the hills and fields, catching butterflies, watching the birds and bees at work, and studying the flowers and trees in the beautiful meadows and woods. Then when winter came, and the days grew cold, they went to school; and in the evening, when the fire was burning brightly, they read and studied in books about all they had seen in the summer.

Besides all these lovely things, and perhaps best of all, they had a very large yard to play in, so large that it took up a whole block, and seemed like a little farm in the middle of the town. There was a lovely lawn and flower beds; a vegetable garden, barnyard and stable; and an orchard where all kinds of fruit trees grew, apple, peach, pear, and many others. A cow lived down in the meadows of clover, and old Bob, the horse, was sometimes turned out to pasture there. But nicest of all, there was the wood yard. You must remember that every winter, where these little girls lived, the snow fell, and lay so deep on the roads that no one could bring in wood from the forest, and without it all the people would have frozen in their cold homes.

So every September the gates were thrown wide open, and into the yard load after load of wood was drawn and piled up under the shed. Then, when it was too cold to play out on the hills, the little girls used to have a fine time in the yard, piling up the wood, making beds, tables, chairs, and stoves of the sticks that had once been the waving branches and strong, sturdy trunks of trees.

Toward spring, they often found a strange yellow powder on the ground under the wood. At first they played with it, calling it flour, and made pies and cakes out of it. But at last they began to wonder where the flour came from, and after watching and studying a long time this is what they found out.

But first I must tell you that all the time the three little girls were happy and busy in this beautiful place, they were not the only family there. There were the robins' children, whose mammas were trying to make them good and happy too. There were the beetles' children, the ants' children, and families of toads, butterflies, and spiders. And while the three little girls were playing with the sticks of wood, there lay, tucked snugly away inside of them, many families of children, warm and safe in their wooden home.

Now I want the smallest of you little children to hold up her hand. How small it is compared with your body! Now let us see the little finger on that hand,— it is smaller still; and now look at the nail on that finger: the brothers and sisters of one of these families were altogether about as large as that tiny nail. Their mamma was a wasp, with light, gauzy wings and a strong body with a long sting on the end of it, about the length of a needle. With this little sting or saw, as it really was, she had bored many holes in the wood when it was still a green tree, and at the bottom of each hole she had laid a tiny egg. There it lay for a long time, all white and still, until one day it cracked open, and out came a funny little white grub, with six short white feet, and black jaws very strong and large for such a tiny thing. This little creature had never had anything to eat, and as it was very hungry indeed, it fell to eating — what do you think? Wood! — its own house! You would n't like a stick of wood for your breakfast, I know, but the wasp-mamma knew what her little grub-children would want, so she put them in just the right place; for they could n't have eaten anything else. And the hungry little grubs ate and ate and ate as long as they could, pushing away from the hole the part they did not want, and this fell upon the ground as the strange yellow powder the children found in the wood-yard, every spring.

And so, while the little girls were playing away in the sunshine the little grubs were eating away in the wood, until at last, one day, they grew satisfied, and one after another went to sleep. There they lay in their dark homes, fast asleep, through long weeks, while the snow was melting and the grass coming up, and the birds and bees beginning their summer work again; until one day these lazy little creatures, that had never done anything in their lives but eat and sleep, woke up and began to stretch themselves. But what had happened to them? Instead of the soft white bodies they had gone to sleep with, they now had black ones and four gauzy wings; while six slender legs had taken the place of the six short ones. There were still the strong black jaws to do all needful work with, and in addition, delicate mouthparts, for their food was now to be the honey from flowers. In fact, they looked and were just like their mamma, the gauzy wasp. One after another they crept to the end of the passage that led from their dark homes to the bright world without. They stood one minute at the little dark hole, and then, spreading their wings, flitted out into the beautiful world of sunshine and flowers.

THE STORY OF CHRISTMAS.

"A great spiritual efficiency lies in story-telling."—
FROEBEL.

CHRISTMAS DAY, you know, dear children, is Christ's day, Christ's birthday, and I want to tell you why we love it so much, and why we try to make every one happy when it comes each year.

A long, long time ago — more than nineteen hundred years — the baby Christ was born on Christmas Day: a baby so wonderful and so beautiful, who grew up to be a man so wise, so good, so patient and sweet, that, every year, the people who know about him love him better and better, and are more and more glad when his birthday comes again. You see that he must have been very good and wonderful; for people have always remembered his birthday, and kept it lovingly for nineteen hundred years.

He was born, long years ago, in a land far, far away across the seas.

Before the baby Christ was born, Mary, his mother, had to make a long journey with her husband, Joseph. They made this journey to be taxed or counted; for in those days this could not be done in the town where people happened to live, but they must be numbered in the place where they were born.

In that far-off time, the only way of traveling was on a horse, or a camel, or a good, patient donkey. Camels and horses cost a great deal of money, and Mary was very poor; so she rode on a quiet, safe donkey, while Joseph walked by her side, leading him and leaning on his stick. Mary was very young, and beautiful, I think, but Joseph was a great deal older than she.

People dress nowadays, in those distant countries, just as they did so many years ago, so we know that Mary must have worn a long, thick dress, falling all about her in heavy folds, and that she had a soft white veil over her head and neck, and across her face. Mary lived in Nazareth, and the journey they were making was to Bethlehem, many miles away.

They were a long time traveling, I am sure; for donkeys are slow, though they are so careful, and Mary must have been very tired before they came to the end of their journey.

They had traveled all day, and it was almost dark when they came near to Bethlehem, to the town where the baby Christ was to be born. There was the place they were to stay,—a kind of inn, or lodging-house, but not at all like those you know about.

They have them to-day in that far-off country, just as they built them so many years ago.

It was a low, flat-roofed, stone building, with no window and only one large door. There were no nicely furnished bedrooms inside, and no soft white beds for the tired travelers; there were only little places built into the stones of the wall, something like the berths on steamboats nowadays, and each traveler brought his own bedding. No pretty garden was in front of the inn, for the road ran close to the very door, so that its dust lay upon the doorsill. All around the house, to a high, rocky hill at the back, a heavy stone fence was built, so that the people and the animals inside might be kept safe.

Mary and Joseph could not get very near the inn; for the whole road in front was filled with camels and donkeys and sheep and cows, while a great many men were going to and fro, taking care of the animals. Some of these people had come to Bethlehem to be counted, as Mary and Joseph had done, and others were staying for the night, on their way to Jerusalem, a large city a little farther on.

The yard was filled, too, with camels and sheep; and men were lying on the ground beside them, resting, and watching, and keeping them safe. The inn was so full and the yard was so full of people, that there was no room for anybody else, and the keeper had to take Joseph and Mary through the house and back to the high hill, where they found another place that was used for a stable. This had only a door and a front, and deep caves were behind, stretching far into the rocks.

This was the spot where Christ was born. Think how poor a place! — but Mary was glad to be there, after all; and when the Christ-child came, he was like other babies, and had so lately come from heaven that he was happy everywhere.

There were mangers all around the cave, where the cattle and sheep were fed, and great heaps of hay and straw were lying on the floor. Then, I think, there were brown-eyed cows and oxen there, and quiet, woolly sheep, and perhaps even some dogs that had come in to take care of the sheep.

And there in the cave, by and by, the wonderful baby came, and they wrapped him up and laid him in a manger.

All the stars in the sky shone brightly that night, for they knew the Christ-child was born, and the angels in heaven sang together for joy. The angels knew about the lovely child, and were glad that he had come to help the people on earth to be good.

There lay the beautiful baby, with a manger for his bed, and oxen and sheep all sleeping quietly round him. His mother watched him and loved him, and by and by many people came to see him, for they had heard that a wonderful child was to be born in Bethlehem. All the people in the inn visited him, and even the shepherds left their flocks in the fields and sought the child and his mother.

But the baby was very tiny, and could not

talk any more than any other tiny child, so he lay in his mother's lap, or in the manger, and only looked at the people. So after they had seen him and loved him, they went away again.

After a time, when the baby had grown larger, Mary took him back to Nazareth, and there he lived and grew up.

And he grew to be such a sweet, wise, loving boy, such a tender, helpful man, and he said so many good and beautiful things, that every one loved him who knew him. Many of the things he said are in the Bible, you know, and a great many beautiful stories of the things he used to do while he was on earth.

He loved little children like you very much, and often used to take them up in his arms and talk to them.

And this is the reason we love Christmas Day so much, and try to make everybody happy when it comes around each year. This is the reason: because Christ, who was born on Christmas Day, has helped us all to be good so many, many times, and because he was the best Christmas present the great world ever had!

THE FIRST THANKSGIVING DAY.

"The story brings forward other people, other relations, other times and places, other and even quite different forms; notwithstanding this fact, the auditor seeks his image there."
— FROEBEL.

NEARLY three hundred years ago, a great many of the people in England were very unhappy because their king would not let them pray to God as they liked. The king said they must use the same prayers that he did; and if they would not do this, they were often thrown into prison, or perhaps driven away from home.

"Let us go away from this country," said the unhappy Englishmen to each other; and so they left their homes, and went far off to a country called Holland. It was about this time that they began to call themselves "Pilgrims." Pilgrims, you know, are people who are always traveling to find something they love, or to find a land where they can be happier; and these English men and women were journeying, they said, "from place to place, toward heaven, their dearest country."

In Holland, the Pilgrims were quiet and happy for a while, but they were very poor; and when the children began to grow up, they were not like English children, but talked Dutch, like the little ones of Holland, and some grew naughty and did not want to go to church any more.

"This will never do," said the Pilgrim fathers and mothers; so after much talking and thinking and writing they made up their minds to come here to America. They hired two vessels, called the Mayflower and the Speedwell, to take them across the sea; but the Speedwell was not a strong ship, and the captain had to take her home again before she had gone very far.

The Mayflower went back, too. Part of the Speedwell's passengers were given to her, and then she started alone across the great ocean.

There were one hundred people on board,— mothers and fathers, brothers and sisters and little children. They were very crowded; it was cold and uncomfortable; the sea was rough, and pitched the Mayflower about, and they were two months sailing over the water.

The children cried many times on the journey, and wished they had never come on the tiresome ship that rocked them so hard, and would not let them keep still a minute.

But they had one pretty plaything to amuse them, for in the middle of the great ocean a Pilgrim baby was born, and they called him "Oceanus," for his birthplace. When the children grew so tired that they were cross and fretful, Oceanus' mother let them come and play with him, and that always brought smiles and happy faces back again.

At last the Mayflower came in sight of land; but if the children had been thinking of grass and flowers and birds, they must have been very much disappointed, for the month was cold November, and there was nothing to be seen but rocks and sand and hard bare ground.

Some of the Pilgrim fathers, with brave Captain Myles Standish at their head, went on shore to see if they could find any houses or white people. But they only saw some wild Indians, who ran away from them, and found some Indian huts and some corn buried in holes in the ground. They went to and fro from the ship three times, till by and by they found a pretty place to live, where there were "fields and little running brooks."

Then at last all the tired Pilgrims landed from the ship on a spot now called Plymouth Rock, and the first house was begun on Christmas Day. But when I tell you how sick they were and how much they suffered that first winter, you will be very sad and sorry for them. The weather was cold, the snow fell fast and thick, the wind was icy, and the Pilgrim fathers had no one to help them cut down the trees and build their church and their houses.

The Pilgrim mothers helped all they could; but they were tired with the long journey, and cold, and hungry too, for no one had the right kind of food to eat, nor even enough of it.

So first one was taken sick, and then another, till half of them were in bed at the same time. Brave Myles Standish and the other soldiers nursed them as well as they knew how; but before spring came half of the people died and had gone at last to "heaven, their dearest country."

But by and by the sun shone more brightly, the snow melted, the leaves began to grow, and sweet spring had come again.

Some friendly Indians had visited the Pilgrims during the winter, and Captain Myles Standish, with several of his men, had returned the visit.

One of the kind Indians was called Squanto, and he came to stay with the Pilgrims, and showed them how to plant their corn, and their pease and wheat and barley.

When the summer came and the days were long and bright, the Pilgrim children were very happy, and they thought Plymouth a lovely place indeed. All kinds of beautiful wild flowers grew at their doors, there were hundreds of birds and butterflies, and the great pine woods were always cool and shady when the sun was too bright.

When it was autumn the fathers gathered the barley and wheat and corn that they had planted, and found that it had grown so well that they would have quite enough for the long winter that was coming.

"Let us thank God for it all," they said. "It is He who has made the sun shine and the rain fall and the corn grow." So they thanked God in their homes and in their little church; the fathers and the mothers and the children thanked Him.

"Then," said the Pilgrim mothers, "let us have a great Thanksgiving party, and invite the friendly Indians, and all rejoice together."

So they had the first Thanksgiving party, and a grand one it was! Four men went out shooting one whole day, and brought back so many wild ducks and geese and great wild turkeys that there was enough for almost a week. There was deer meat also, of course, for there were plenty of fine deer in the forest. Then the Pilgrim mothers made the corn and wheat into bread and cakes, and they had fish and clams from the sea besides.

The friendly Indians all came with their chief Massasoit. Every one came that was invited, and more, I dare say, for there were ninety of them altogether.

They brought five deer with them, that they gave to the Pilgrims; and they must have liked the party very much, for they stayed three days.

Kind as the Indians were, you would have been very much frightened if you had seen them; and the baby Oceanus, who was a year old then, began to cry at first whenever they came near him.

They were dressed in deerskins, and some of them had the furry coat of a wild cat hanging on their arms. Their long black hair fell loose on their shoulders, and was trimmed with feathers or fox-tails. They had their faces painted in all kinds of strange ways, some with black stripes as broad as your finger all up and down them. But whatever they wore, it was their very best, and they had put it on for the Thanksgiving party.

Each meal, before they ate anything, the Pilgrims and the Indians thanked God together for all his goodness. The Indians sang and danced in the evenings, and every day they ran races and played all kinds of games with the children.

Then sometimes the Pilgrims with their guns, and the Indians with their bows and arrows, would see who could shoot farthest and best. So they were glad and merry and thankful for three whole days.

THE FIRST THANKSGIVING DAY.

The Pilgrim mothers and fathers had been sick and sad many times since they landed from the Mayflower; they had worked very hard, often had not had enough to eat, and were mournful indeed when their friends died and left them. But now they tried to forget all this, and think only of how good God had been to them; and so they all were happy together at the first Thanksgiving party.

· · · · · · ·

All this happened nearly three hundred years ago, and ever since that time Thanksgiving has been kept in our country.

Every year our fathers and grandfathers and great-grandfathers have "rejoiced together" like the Pilgrims, and have had something to be thankful for each time.

Every year some father has told the story of the brave Pilgrims to his little sons and daughters, and has taught them to be very glad and proud that the Mayflower came sailing to our country so many years ago.

LITTLE GEORGE WASHINGTON.

PART I.

"The child takes each story as a conquest, grasps each as a treasure, and inserts into his own life, for his own advancement and instruction, what each story teaches and shows."— FROEBEL.

EVERY one of my little children has seen a picture of George Washington, I am sure.

Perhaps you may remember his likeness on a prancing white horse, holding his cocked hat in his hand, and bowing low to the people, or his picture as a general at the head of his armies, with a sword by his side and high boots reaching to the knee; sometimes you have seen him in a boat crossing the Delaware River, wrapped in his heavy soldier's cloak; and again as a President, with powdered hair, lace ruffles, and velvet coat.

Of course all these are pictures of a strong, handsome, grown-up man, and I suppose you never happened to think that George Washington was once a little boy.

But ever so long ago he was as small as you are now, and I am going to tell you about his father and mother, his home and his little-boy days.

He was born one hundred and sixty years ago in Virginia, near a great river called the Potomac. His father's name was Augustine, his mother's Mary, and he had several brothers and a little sister.

They all lived in the country on a farm, or a plantation, as they call it in Virginia. The Washington house stood in the middle of green tobacco fields and flowery meadows, and there were so many barns and storehouses and sheds round about it that they made quite a village of themselves. The nearest neighbors lived miles away; there were no railroads nor stages, and if you wanted to travel, you must ride on horseback through the thick woods, or you might sail in little boats up and down the rivers.

City boys and girls might think, perhaps, that little George Washington was very lonely on the great plantation, with no neighbor-boys to play with; but you must remember that the horses and cattle and sheep and dogs on a farm make the dearest of playmates, and that there are all kinds of pleasant things to do in the country that city boys know nothing about.

Little George played out of doors all the time and grew very strong. He went fishing and swimming in the great river, he ran races and jumped fences with his brothers and the dogs, he threw stones across the brooks, and when he grew a larger boy he even learned to shoot.

He had a pretty pony, too, named "Hero," that he loved very much, and that he used to ride all about the plantation.

Some of the letters have been kept that he wrote when he was a little boy, and he talks in them about his pony, and his books with pictures of elephants, and the new top he is going to have soon.

Think of that great General Washington on a white horse once playing with a little humming top like yours!

Many things are told about Washington when he was little; but he lived so long ago that we cannot tell very well whether they ever happened or not. One story is that his father took him out into the garden on a spring morning, and drew the letters of his name with a cane in the soft earth. Then he filled the letters with seed, and told little George to wait a week or two and see what would happen. You can all guess what did happen, and can think how pleased the little boy was when he found his name all growing in fresh green leaves.

Then another story, I'm sure you've all heard, is about the cherry-tree and the hatchet.

Little George's father gave him one day, so they say, a nice, bright, sharp little hatchet. Of course he went around the barns and the sheds, trying everything and seeing how well he could cut, and at last he went into the orchard. There he saw a young cherry-tree, as straight as a soldier, with the most beautiful, smooth, shining bark, waving its boughs in a very provoking way, as if to say, "You can't cut me down, and you need n't try."

Little George did try and he did cut it down, and then was very sorry, for he found it was not so easy to set it up again.

"THE LETTERS OF HIS NAME . . . IN THE SOFT EARTH" (page 118)

His father was angry, of course, for he lived in a new country, and three thousand miles from any place where he could get good fruit trees; but when the little boy told the truth about it, his father said he would rather lose a thousand cherry-trees than have his son tell a lie.

Now perhaps this never happened; but if George Washington ever did cut down a cherry-tree, you may be sure he told the truth about it.

I think, though he grew to be such a wise, wonderful man, that he must have been just a bright, happy boy like you, when he was little.

But everybody knows three things about him, — that he always told the truth, that he never was afraid of anything, and that he always loved and minded his mother.

When little George was eleven years old, his good father died, and his poor mother was left alone to take care of her boys and her great plantation. What a busy mother she was! She mended and sewed, she taught some of her children, she took care of the sick people, she spun wool and knitted stockings and gloves; but every day she found time to gather her children around her and read good books to them, and talk to them about being good children.

So riding his pony, and helping his mother, and learning his lessons, George grew to be a tall boy.

When he was fourteen years old, he made up his mind that he would like to be a sailor, and travel far away over the blue water in a great ship. His elder brother said that he might do so. The right ship was found; his clothes were packed and carried on board, when all at once his mother said he must not go. She had thought about it; he was too young to go away, and she wanted her boy to stay with her.

Of course George was greatly disappointed, but he stayed at home, and worked and studied hard. He wanted very much to learn how to earn money and help his mother, and so he studied to be a surveyor.

Surveyors measure the land, you know. They measure people's gardens and house-lots and farms, and can tell just where to put the fences, and how much land belongs to you and how much to me, so that we need never quarrel about it.

To be a good surveyor you have to be very careful indeed, and make no mistakes; and George Washington was careful and always tried to do his best, so that his surveys were the finest that could be made.

When he was only sixteen, he went off into the great forest, where no one lived but the Indians, to measure some land for a friend of his. The weather was cold; he slept in a tent at night, or out of doors, on a bearskin by the fire, and he had to work very hard. He met a great many Indians, and learned to know their ways in fighting and how to manage them.

Three years he worked hard at surveying, and at last he was a grown-up man!

He was tall and splendid then, over six feet high, and as straight as an Indian, with a rosy face and bright blue eyes. He had large hands and fingers, and was wonderfully strong. People say that his great tent, which it took three men to carry, Washington could lift with one hand and throw into the wagon.

He was very brave, too, you remember. He

could shoot well, and almost never missed his aim; he was used to walking many miles when he was surveying, and he could ride any horse he liked, no matter how wild and fierce.

So you see, when a man is strong, when he can shoot well, and walk and ride great distances, when he is never afraid of anything, that is just the man for a soldier; and I will tell you soon how George Washington came to be a great soldier.

GREAT GEORGE WASHINGTON.

PART II.

"The good story-teller effects much; he has an ennobling effect upon children, — so much the more ennobling that he does not appear to intend it." — FROEBEL.

ALL this time while George Washington had been growing up, — first a little boy, then a larger boy, and then a young surveyor, — all this time the French and English and Indians were unhappy and uncomfortable in the country north of Virginia. The French wanted all the land, so did the English, and the Indians saw that there would be no room for them, whichever had it, so they all began to trouble each other and to quarrel and fight.

These troubles grew so bad at last that the Virginians began to be afraid of the French and Indians, and thought they must have some soldiers of their own ready to fight.

George Washington was only nineteen then, but everybody knew he was wise and brave, so they chose him to teach the soldiers near his home how to march and to fight.

Then the king and the people of England grew very uneasy at all this quarreling, and they sent over soldiers and cannon and powder, and commenced to get ready to fight in earnest. Washington was made a major, and he had to go a thousand miles, in the middle of winter, into the Indian and French country, to see the chiefs and the soldiers, and find out about the troubles.

When he came back again, all the people were so pleased with his courage and with the wise way in which he had behaved, that they made him lieutenant-colonel.

Then began a long war between the French and the English, which lasted seven years. Washington fought through all of it, and was made a colonel, and by and by commander of all the soldiers in Virginia. He built forts and roads, he gained and lost battles, he fought the Indians and the French; and by all this trouble and hard work he learned to be a great soldier.

In many of the battles of this war, Washington and the Virginians did not wear a uniform like the English soldiers, but a buckskin shirt and fringed leggings like the Indians.

From beginning to end of some of the battles, Washington rode about among the men, telling them where to go and how to fight; the bullets were whistling around him all the time, but he said he liked the music.

By and by the war was over; the French were driven back to their own part of the country, and Washington went home to Mt. Vernon to rest, and took with him his wife, lovely Martha Washington, whom he had met and married while he was fighting the French and Indians.

While he was at Mt. Vernon he saw all his horses again, — "Valiant" and "Magnolia" and "Chinkling" and "Ajax," — and had grand gallops over the country.

He had some fine dogs, too, to run by his side, and help him hunt the bushy-tailed foxes. "Vulcan" and "Ringwood" and "Music" and "Sweetlips" were the names of some of them. You may be sure the dogs were glad when they had their master home again.

But Washington did not have long to rest, for another war was coming, the great war of the Revolution.

Little children cannot understand all the reasons for this war, but I can tell you some of them.

You remember in the story of Thanksgiving I told you about the Pilgrim fathers, who came from England to this country because their king would not let them pray to God as they liked. That king was dead now, and there was another in his place, a king with the name of George, like our Washington.

Now our great-grandfathers had always loved England and Englishmen, because many of their friends were still living there, and because it was their old home.

The king gave them governors to help take care of their people, and soldiers to fight for them, and they sent to England for many things to wear and to eat.

But just before this Revolutionary War, the king and the great men who helped him began to say that things should be done in this country that our people did not think right at all. The king said they must buy expensive stamps to put on all their newspapers and almanacs and lawyer's papers, and that they must pay very high taxes on their tea and paper and glass, and he sent soldiers to see that this was done.

This made our great-grandfathers very angry. They refused to pay the taxes, they would not buy anything from England any more, and some men even went on board the ships, as they came into Boston Harbor, and threw the tea over into the water.

So fifty-one men were chosen from all over the country, and they met at Philadelphia, to see what could be done. Washington was sent from Virginia. And after they had talked very solemnly, they all thought there would be great trouble soon, and Washington went home to drill the soldiers.

Then the war began with the battle of Lexington, in New England, and soon Washington was made commander in chief of the armies.

He rode the whole distance from Philadelphia to Boston on horseback, with a troop of officers; and all the people on the way came to see him, bringing bands of music and cheering him as he went by. He rode into camp in the morning. The soldiers were drawn up in the road, and men and women and children who had come to look at Washington were crowded all about. They saw a tall, splendid, handsome man in a blue coat with buff facings, and epaulets on his shoulders. As he took off his hat, drew his shining sword and raised it in sight of all the people, the cannon began to thunder, and all the people hurrahed and tossed their hats in the air.

Of course he looked very splendid, and they all knew how brave he was, and thought he would soon put an end to the war.

But it did not happen as they expected, for this was only the beginning, and the war lasted seven long years.

Fighting is always hard, even if you have plenty of soldiers and plenty for them to eat; but Washington had very few soldiers, and very little powder for the guns, and little food for the men to eat.

The soldiers were not in uniform, as ours are to-day; but each was dressed just as he happened to come from his shop or his farm.

Washington ordered hunting shirts for them, such as he wore when he went to fight the Indians, for he knew they would look more like soldiers if all were dressed alike.

Of course many people thought that our men would be beaten, as the war went on; but Washington never thought so, for he was sure our side was right.

I hardly know what he would have done, at last, if the French people had not promised to come over and help us, and to send us money and men and ships. All the people in the army thanked God when they heard it, and fired their guns for joy.

A brave young man named Lafayette came with the French soldiers, and he grew to be Washington's great friend, and fought for us all through the Revolution.

Many battles were fought in this war, and Washington lost some of them, and a great many of his men were killed.

You could hardly understand how much trouble he had. In the winter, when the snow was deep on the ground, he had no houses or huts for his men to sleep in; his soldiers were ragged and cold by day, and had not blankets enough to keep them warm by night; their shoes were old and worn, and they had to wrap cloths around their feet to keep them from freezing.

When they marched to the Delaware River, one cold Christmas night, a soldier who was sent after them, with a message for Washington, traced them by their footprints on the snow, all reddened with the blood from their poor cut feet.

They must have been very brave and patient to have fought at all, when they were so cold and ragged and hungry.

Washington suffered a great deal in seeing his soldiers so wretched, and I am sure that, with all his strength and courage, he would sometimes have given up hope, if he had not talked and prayed to God a great deal, and asked Him to help him.

In one of the hardest times of the whole war, Washington was staying at a farmer's house. One morning, he rode out very early to visit the soldiers. The farmer went into the fields soon after, and as he was passing a brook where a great many bushes were growing, he heard a deep voice from the thicket. He looked through the leaves, and saw Washington on his knees, on the ground, praying to God for his soldiers. He had fastened his horse to a tree, and come away by himself to ask God to help them.

At last the war came to an end; the English were beaten, and our armies sent up praise and thanks to God.

Then the soldiers went quietly back to their homes, and Washington bade all his officers good-by, and thanked them for their help and their courage.

The little room in New York where he said farewell is kept to show to visitors now, and you can see it some day yourselves.

Then Washington went home to Mt. Vernon to rest; but before he had been there long, the people found out that they must have some one to help take care of them, as they had nothing to do with the king of England any more; and they asked Washington to come and be the first President of the United States.

So he did as they wished, and was as wise and good, and as careful and fine a President as he had been surveyor, soldier, and general.

You know we always call Washington the Father of his Country, because he did so much for us and helped to make the United States so great.

After he died, there were parks and mountains and villages and towns and cities named for him all over the land, because people loved him so and prized so highly what he had done for them.

In the city of Washington there is a building where you can see many of the things that belonged to the first President, when he was alive. There is his soldier's coat, his sword, and in an old camp chest are the plates and knives and forks that he used in the Revolution.

There is a tall, splendid monument of shining gray stone in that city, that towers far, far above all the highest roofs and spires. It was built in memory of George Washington, by the people of the United States, to show that they loved and would always remember the Father of his Country.

THE MAPLE-LEAF AND THE VIOLET.

"Story-telling must please children, so that it will influence, strengthen, and elevate their lives." — FROEBEL.

THE Maple-tree lived on the edge of the wood. Beside and behind her the trees grew so thick and tall that there was plenty of shade at her roots; but as no one stood in front, she could always look across the meadows to the brown house where Bessie lived, and could see what went on in the world.

After the cold winter had gone by, and the spring had come again, the Maple-tree sent out thousands of tiny leaf-buds, that stretched themselves, and grew larger day by day in the warm sunshine. One little Bud, on the end of a tall branch, worked so hard to grow that by and by he finished opening all his folds, and found himself a tiny pale green leaf.

He was curious, as little folks generally are,

and as soon as he opened his eyes wanted to see everything about him. First he looked up at the blue sky overhead, but the sky only looked quietly back at him. Then he looked across the meadows to where Bessie lived, but Bessie was at school and the house was still.

Then he gazed far down below him on the ground; and there, just beneath, was a little Violet. She had uncurled her purple petals a few days before, and was waiting to welcome the first leaf-bud that came out.

So when the Maple-leaf looked down, she smiled up at him and said, "Good-morning." He answered her politely, but he was very little, and did not know quite what to say, so he didn't talk any more that day.

The next morning they greeted each other again, and soon they grew to be good friends, and talked together very happily all day. The Maple-leaf lived so high up in the tree that he could easily see across the fields, and he watched every day for Bessie as she started for school. When she came out of her door, he told the Violet, and the Violet always said every morning, "Dear Bessie! I should like to see her, too!"

Sometimes, when the day was chilly and it was almost too damp in the shade, the Violet used to wish she might be high up on the branch above her, waving about in the sunshine like the Maple-leaf; but she was a contented little thing, and never fretted long for what she could not have.

It was generally pleasant on the ground, and the bugs and caterpillars and worms, as they crawled about at her roots, often told her very interesting things about their families and their troubles.

One day it was very dry and warm. The Maple-leaf was not at all comfortable, high in the hot air, and he said to his mother, "Mother-tree, won't you let me go down by the Violet and be cool?"

Then the Maple-tree answered, "No, no, little leaf, not now; if I once let you go, you can never come back again. Stay quietly here; the time will soon come for you to leave me."

The Maple-leaf told this to the Violet, and then they began to fear that when the mother-tree let him go, by and by, he might not be able to fall close beside the Violet.

So the next day, when the wind came whistling along, the Violet asked him if he would kindly take care of the leaf, and send him to her when the mother-tree let him go. The wind was rough and careless, and said he really did n't know. He could n't be sure how he'd feel then. They would have to wait and see.

The two little friends were rather unhappy about this, but they waited quietly. By and by the weather grew cold. The air was so chill that the Maple-leaf shivered in the night, and in the morning, when the sun rose, and he could see himself, he found he was all red, just as your hands and cheeks are on a frosty morning. When the mother-tree saw him, she told him he would soon leave her now, and she bade him good-by. He was sorry to go, but then he thought of his dear Violet, and was happy again.

By and by a gust of cold wind came blowing by, and twisted the little leaf about, and fluttered him so that he could not hold to the tree any longer. So at last he blew off, and the wind took him up and danced with him and played with him until he was very tired and dizzy. But at last, for he was a kind wind after all, he blew the leaf back, straight to the side of the Violet. How close they cuddled to each other, and how happy they were! You would have been very glad if you had seen them together.

In the morning, when the sun rose yellow and bright, Bessie came into the woods with a basket and a trowel. It was nearly winter, and she knew that soon the snow would fall and cover all the pretty growing things. So she dug up, very carefully, roots of plumy fern and partridge berries with their leaves, and wintergreen and boxberry plants, to grow in her window-garden in the winter. She took the Violet too, bringing away so much of the earth around her roots that the little thing scarcely felt that she had been moved. As Bessie put her plants in the basket, she saw the little Maple-leaf resting close by the violet, but he looked so pretty, lying there, that she did not move him.

In the sunny window of the little brown house the Violet grew still more fresh and green. But each day, as the plants were watered, the Maple-leaf curled up a little more at the edges, and sank down farther into the earth, until soon he was almost out of sight, and by and by crumbled quite away. Still he was close beside his Violet, and all the strength he had he gave to her roots.

She always loved him just the same, though she could not see him any longer, and by and by, when she had lived her life, and her leaves withered away, each one, as it fell from the stem, sank into the earth where the Maple-leaf lay.

MRS. CHINCHILLA.

THE TALE OF A CAT.

"See what joyous faces, what shining eyes, and what glad jubilee welcome the story-teller, and what a blooming circle of glad children press around him!" — FROEBEL.

MRS. CHINCHILLA was not a lovely lady, with a dress of soft gray cloth and a great chinchilla muff and boa. Not at all. Mrs. Chinchilla was a beautiful cat, with sleek fur like silver-gray satin, and a very handsome tail to match, quite long enough to brush the ground when she walked. She did n't live in a house, but she had a very comfortable home in a fine drug-store, with one large bay-window almost to herself and her kittens. She had three pretty fat dumplings of kittens, all in soft shades of gray like their mother. She did n't like any other color in kittens so well as a quiet ladylike gray. None of her children ever were black, or white, or yellow, but sometimes they had four snow-white socks on their gray paws. Mrs. Chinchilla did n't mind that, for white socks were really a handsome finish to a gray kitten, though, of course, it was a deal of trouble to keep them clean.

At the time my story begins the kits were all tiny catkins, whose eyes had been open only a day or two, so Mrs. Chinchilla had to wash them every morning herself. She had the most wonderful tongue! I'll tell you what that tongue had in it: a hair-brush, a comb, a tooth-brush, a nail-brush, a sponge, a towel, and a cake of soap! And when Mrs. Chinchilla had finished those three little catkins, they were as fresh and sweet, and shiny and clean, and kissable and huggable, as any baby just out of a bath-tub.

One morning, just after the little kits had had their scrub in the sunny bay-window, they felt, all at once, old enough to play; and so they began to scramble over each other, and run about between the great colored glass jars, and even to chase and bite the ends of their own tails. They had not known that they had any tails before that morning, and of course it was a charming surprise. Mrs.

Chinchilla looked on lazily and gravely. It had been a good while since she had had time or had felt young and gay enough to chase *her* tail, but she was very glad to see the kittens enjoy themselves harmlessly.

Now, while this was going on, some one came up to the window and looked in. It was the Boy who lived across the street. Mrs. Chinchilla disliked nearly all boys, but she was afraid of this one. He had golden curls and a Fauntleroy collar, and the sweetest lips that ever said prayers, and clean dimpled hands that looked as if they had been made to stroke cats and make them purr. But instead of stroking them he rubbed their fur the wrong way, and hung tin kettles to their tails, and tied handkerchiefs over their heads. When Mrs. Chinchilla saw the Boy she humped her back, so that it looked like a gray mountain, and said, "Sftt!" three times. When the Boy found that she was looking at him, and lashing her tail, and yawning so as to show him her sharp white teeth, he suddenly disappeared from sight. So Mrs. Chinchilla gave the kittens their breakfast, and they cuddled themselves into a round ball, and went fast asleep. They were first rolled so tightly, and then so tied up with their tails, that you couldn't have told whether they were three or six little catkins. When their soft *purr-r-r-r*, *purr-r-r-r* had first changed into sleepy little snores, and then died away altogether, Mrs. Chinchilla jumped down out of the window, and went for her morning airing in the back yard. At the same time the druggist passed behind a tall desk to mix some medicine, and the shop was left alone.

Just then the Boy (for he hadn't gone away at all; he had just stooped out of sight) rushed in the door quickly, snatched one of the kittens out of the round ball, and ran away with it as fast as he could run. Pretty soon Mrs. Chinchilla came back, and of course she counted the kittens the very first thing. She always did it. To her surprise and fright she found only two instead of three. She knew she couldn't be mistaken. There were five kittens in her last family, and two less in this family; and five kittens less two kittens is three kittens. One chinchilla catkin gone! What should she do?

She had once heard a lady say that there

were too many cats in the world already, but she had no patience with people who made such wicked speeches. Her kittens had always been so beautiful that they sometimes sold for fifty cents apiece, and none of them had ever been drowned.

Mrs. Chinchilla knew in a second just where that kitten had gone. It makes a pussy-cat very quick and bright and wise to take care of and train large families of frisky kittens, with very little help from their father in bringing them up. She knew that that Boy had carried off the kitten, and she intended to have it back, and scratch the Boy with some long scratches, if she could only get the chance. Looking at her claws, she found them nice and sharp, and as the druggist opened the door for a customer Mrs. Chinchilla slipped out, with just one backward glance, as much as to say, "Gone out; will be back soon." Then she dashed across the street, and waited on the steps of the Boy's house. Very soon a man came with a bundle, and when the housemaid opened the door Mrs. Chinchilla walked in. She had n't any visiting-card with her; but then the Boy had n't left any card when he called for the kitten, so she did n't care for that.

The housemaid did n't see her when she slipped in. It was a very nice house to hold such a heartless boy, she thought. The parlor door was open, but she knew the kitten would n't be there, so she ran upstairs. When she reached the upper hall she stood perfectly still, with her ears up and her whiskers trembling. Suddenly she heard a faint mew, then another, and then a laugh; that was the Boy. She pushed open a door that was ajar, and walked into the nursery. The Boy was seated in the middle of the floor, tying the kitten to a tin cart, and the poor little thing was mewing piteously. Mrs. Chinchilla dashed up to the Boy, scratched him as many long scratches as she had time for at that moment, took the frightened kitten in her kind, gentle mouth, the way all mother-cats do (because if they carried them in their forepaws they would n't have enough left to walk on), and was downstairs and out on the front doorstep before the housemaid had finished paying the man for the bundle. And when she got that chinchilla catkin home in the safe, sunny bay-win dow, she washed it over and over and over so many times that it never forgot, so long as it lived, the day it was stolen by the Boy.

When the Boy's mother hurried upstairs to see why he was crying so loud, she told him that he must expect to be scratched by mother-cats if he stole their kittens. "I shall take your pretty Fauntleroy collar off," she said; "it does n't match your disposition."

The Boy cried bitterly until luncheon time, but when he came to think over the matter, he knew that his mother was right, and Mrs. Chinchilla was right, too; so he treated all mother-cats and their kittens more kindly after that.

A STORY OF THE FOREST.

"It is not the gay forms he meets in the fairy-tale which charm the child, but a spiritual, invisible truth lying far deeper." — FROEBEL.

FAR away, in the depths of a great green rustling wood, there lived a Fir-tree. She was tall and dark and fragrant; so tall that her topmost plumes seemed waving about in the clouds, and her branches were so thick and strong and close set that down below them on the ground it was dark almost as night.

There were many other trees in the forest, as tall and grand as she, and when they bent and bowed to each other, as the wind played in their branches, you could hear a wonderful lovely sound, like the great organ when it plays softly in the church.

Down below, under the trees, the ground was covered with a glossy brown carpet of the sharp, needle-like leaves the fir-trees had let fall, and on this carpet there were pointed brown fir cones lying, looking dry and withered, and yet bearing under their scales many little seeds, hidden away like very precious letters in their dainty envelopes.

Even on bright summer days this wood was cool and dark, and, as you walked about on the soft brown carpet, you could hear the wonderful song the pine needles made as they rubbed against each other; and perhaps far away in the top of some tall tree you could hear the wood-thrush sing out gladly.

All around the great Fir-tree, where her cones had dropped, a family of young firs was growing up, — very tiny yet, so tiny you might have crushed them as you walked, and not felt them under your foot.

The Fir-tree spread her thick branches over them, and kept off the fierce wind and the bitter cold, and under her shelter they were growing strong.

They were all fine little trees, but one of them, that stood quite apart from the rest, was the finest of all, very straight and well shaped and handsome. Every day he looked up at the mother-tree, and saw how straight and strong she grew, — how the wind bent and waved her branches, but did not stir her great trunk; and as he looked, he sent his own rootlets farther down into the dark earth, and held his tiny head up more proudly.

The other trees did not all try to grow strong and tall. Indeed, one of them said, "Why should I try to grow? Who can see me here in this dark wood? What good will it do for me to try? I can never be as fine and strong as the mother-tree."

So he was unhappy and hung his head, and let the wind blow him further and further over toward the ground; and as he did not care for his rootlets, they lost their hold in the earth, and by and by he withered quite away.

But our brave little Fir-tree grew on; and when a long time had gone by, his head was on a level with his mother's lowest branches, and he could listen and hear all the whispering and talking that went on among the great trees. So he learned many things, for the trees were old and wise; and the birds, who are such great travelers, had told them many wonderful things that had happened in far-off lands.

And the Fir-tree asked his mother many, many questions. "Dear mother-tree," he said, "shall we always live here? Shall I keep on growing until I am a grand tall tree like you? And will you always be with me?"

"Who knows!" said the mother-tree, rustling in all her branches. "If we are stouthearted, and grow strong in trunk and perfect in shape, then perhaps we shall be taken away from the forest and made useful somewhere, — and we want to be useful, little son."

It was about this time that the young Fir-tree made himself some music that he used to whisper when the winds blew and rocked his branches. This is the little song, but I cannot sing it as he did.

SONG OF THE FIR-TREE.

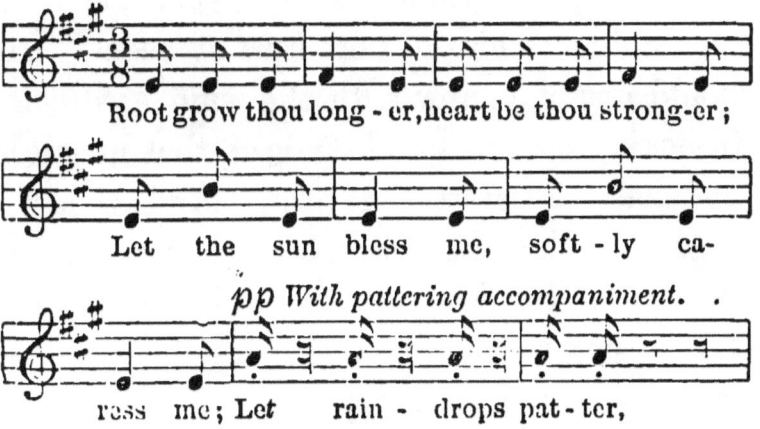

wind, my leaves scatter. My root must grow longer, my heart must grow stronger.

"Root, grow thou longer,
Heart, be thou stronger;
Let the sun bless me,
Softly caress me;
Let raindrops patter,
Wind, my leaves scatter.
My root must grow longer,
My heart must grow stronger."

And one day, when he was singing this song to himself, some birds fluttered near, pleased with the music, and as he seemed kind they began to build their nest in his branches.

Then what a proud Fir-tree, that the birds should choose him to take care of them! He would not play now with the wind as it came frolicking by, but stood straight, that he might not shake the pretty soft nest. And when the eggs were laid at last, all his leaves stroked each other for joy, and the noise they made was so sweet that the mother-tree bent over to see why he was so happy.

The mother-bird sat patiently on the nest all day, and when, now and then, she flew away to rest her tired little legs, the father-bird came to keep the eggs warm.

So the Fir-tree was never alone; and now he asked the birds some of the many questions he had once asked his mother. "Tell me, dear birdies," he said, "what does the mother-tree mean? She says if I grow strong, I shall be taken away to be useful somewhere. How can a Fir-tree be useful if he is taken away from the forest where he was born?"

So the birds told him how he could be useful: how perhaps men might take him for the mast of a ship, and fasten to him, strong and firm, the great white sails that send the ship like a bird over the water; or that he might be used to hold a bright flag, as it waved in the wind. Then the mother-bird thought of the happy Christmas time, for the birds and flowers and trees know all about it; and she told the Fir of the Christmas greens that were cut in the forest; of the branches and boughs that were used to make the houses fresh and bright; and of the Christmas trees, on which gifts were hung for the children.

Now the Fir-tree had seen some children one day, and he knew about their bright eyes, and their rosy cheeks, and their dear soft little hands. The day they came into the woods, they had made a ring and danced about him, and one little girl had held up her finger, and asked the others to hush and hear the song he was singing.

So of all the things the birds had told him, the sweetest to him was about the Christmas tree. If only he might be a Christmas tree, and have the children dance about him again, and feel their presents among his green branches!

So he did all that a little tree could do to grow strong in every part, and each day he sang his song: —

> "Root, grow thou longer,
> Heart, grow thou stronger;
> Sweet sunshine, bless me,
> Softly caress me;
> Cold raindrops, patter,
> Wind, my leaves scatter.
> My roots must grow longer,
> My heart must grow stronger."

Soon the days began to grow cold. The birdlings who had been born in the Fir-tree's branches had gone far away to the South. The father and mother bird had gone too, and on the way had stopped to say good-by to the brave little tree.

The white snow had fallen in gentle flakes, and covered the cones and the glossy carpet of pine needles. All was still and shining and cold in the forest, and the great trees seemed taller and darker than ever.

One day some men came into the wood with saws and ropes and axes, and cut down many of the great trees, and among these was the mother-fir. They fastened oxen to all the trees, and dragged them away, rustling and waving, over the smooth snow.

The mother-tree had gone, — "gone to be useful," said the little Fir; and though he missed her very much, and the world seemed very empty when he looked up and no longer saw her thick branches and her strong trunk, yet he was not unhappy, for he was a brave little Fir.

Still the days grew colder, and often the Fir-tree wondered if the children who had made a ring and danced about him would remember him when Christmas time came.

He could not grow, for the weather was too cold, and so he had the more time for thinking. He thought of the birds, of the mother-tree, and, most of all, of the little girl who had lifted her finger, and said, "Hush! hear the Fir-tree sing."

Sometimes the days seemed long, and he sighed in all his branches, and almost thought he would never be a Christmas tree.

But suddenly, one day, he heard something far away that sounded like the ringing of Christmas bells. It was the children laughing and singing, as they ran over the snow.

Nearer they came, and stood beside the Fir. "Yes," said the little girl, "it is my very tree, my very singing tree!"

"Indeed," said the father, "it will be a good Christmas tree. See how straight and well shaped it is."

Then the tree was glad; not proud, for he was a good little Fir, but glad that they saw he had tried his best.

So they cut him down and carried him away on a great sled; away from the tall dark trees, from the white shining snow-carpet at their

"'NOT ALL FIRS CAN BE CHRISTMAS TREES'" (page 155)

feet, and from all the murmuring and whispering that go on within the forest.

The little trees stood on tiptoe and waved their green branches for "Good-by," and the great trees bent their heads to watch him go.

"Not all firs can be Christmas trees," said they; "only those who grow their best."

. . . .

The good Fir-tree stood in the children's own room. Round about his feet were flowers and mosses and green boughs. From his branches hung toys and books and candies, and at the end of each glossy twig was a bright glittering Christmas candle.

The doors were slowly opened; the children came running in; and when they saw the shining lights, and the Christmas tree proudly holding their presents, they made a ring, and danced about him, singing.

And the Fir-tree was very happy!

PICCOLA.

SUGGESTED BY ONE OF MRS. CELIA THAXTER'S POEMS.

———•———

"Story-telling is a real strengthening spirit-bath." — FROEBEL.

PICCOLA lived in Italy, where the oranges grow, and where all the year the sun shines warm and bright. I suppose you think Piccola a very strange name for a little girl; but in her country it was not strange at all, and her mother thought it the sweetest name a little girl ever had.

Piccola had no kind father, no big brother or sister, and no sweet baby to play with and to love. She and her mother lived all alone in an old stone house that looked on a dark, narrow street. They were very poor, and the mother was away from home almost every day, washing clothes and scrubbing floors, and working hard to earn money for her little girl and herself. So you see Piccola was alone a great deal of the time; and if she had not been a very happy, contented little child, I hardly know what she would have done. She had no playthings except a heap of stones in the back yard that she used for building houses, and a very old, very ragged doll that her mother had found in the street one day.

But there was a small round hole in the stone wall at the back of her yard, and her greatest pleasure was to look through that into her neighbor's garden. When she stood on a stone, and put her eyes close to the hole, she could see the green grass in the garden, smell the sweet flowers, and even hear the water plashing into the fountain. She had never seen any one walking in the garden, for it belonged to an old gentleman who did not care about grass and flowers.

One day in the autumn her mother told her that the old gentleman had gone away, and had rented his house to a family of little American children, who had come with their sick mother to spend the winter in Italy. After this, Piccola was never lonely, for all day long the children ran and played and danced and sang in the garden. It was several weeks before they saw her at all, and I am not sure they would ever have done so but that one day the kitten ran away, and in chasing her they came close to the wall, and saw Piccola's black eyes looking through the hole in the stones. They were a little frightened at first, and did not speak to her; but the next day she was there again, and Rose, the oldest girl, went up to the wall and talked to her a little while. When the children found that she had no one to play with and was very lonely, they talked to her every day, and often brought her fruits and candies, and passed them through the hole in the wall.

One day they even pushed the kitten through; but the hole was hardly large enough for her, and she mewed and scratched, and was very much frightened. After that the little boy said he should ask his father if the hole might not be made larger, and then Piccola could come in and play with them. The father had found out that Piccola's mother was a good woman, and that the little girl herself was sweet and kind, so that he was very glad to have some of the stones broken away, and an opening made for Piccola to come in.

How excited she was, and how glad the children were when she first stepped into the garden! She wore her best dress, a long bright-colored woolen skirt and a white waist. Round her neck was a string of beads, and on her feet were little wooden shoes. It would seem very strange to us — would it not? — to wear wooden shoes; but Piccola and her mother had never worn anything else, and never had any money to buy stockings. Piccola almost always ran about barefooted, like the kittens and the chickens and the little ducks. What a good time they had that day, and how glad Piccola's mother was that her little girl could have such a pleasant, safe place to play in, while she was away at work!

By and by December came, and the little Americans began to talk about Christmas. One day, when Piccola's curly head and bright eyes came peeping through the hole in the wall, they ran to her and helped her in; and as they did so, they all asked her at once what she thought she would have for a Christmas present. " A Christmas present! " said Piccola. " Why, what is that? "

All the children looked surprised at this, and Rose said, rather gravely, "Dear Piccola, don't you know what Christmas is?"

Oh, yes, Piccola knew it was the happy day when the baby Christ was born, and she had been to church on that day, and heard the beautiful singing, and had seen a picture of the Babe lying in the manger, with cattle and sheep sleeping round about. Oh, yes, she knew all that very well, but what was a Christmas present?

Then the children began to laugh, and to answer her all together. There was such a clatter of tongues that she could hear only a few words now and then, such as "chimney," "Santa Claus," "stockings," "reindeer," "Christmas Eve," "candies and toys." Piccola put her hands over her ears, and said, "Oh, I can't understand one word. You tell me, Rose." Then Rose told her all about jolly old Santa Claus, with his red cheeks and white beard and fur coat, and about his reindeer and sleigh full of toys. "Every Christmas Eve," said Rose, "he comes down the chimney, and fills the stockings of all the good children; so, Piccola, you hang up your stocking, and who knows what a beautiful Christmas present you will find when morning comes!" Of course Piccola thought this was a delightful plan, and was very pleased to hear about it. Then all the children told her of every Christmas Eve they could remember, and of the presents they had had; so that she went home thinking of nothing but dolls, and hoops, and balls, and ribbons, and marbles, and wagons, and kites.

She told her mother about Santa Claus, and her mother seemed to think that perhaps he did not know there was any little girl in that house, and very likely he would not come at all. But Piccola felt very sure Santa Claus would remember her, for her little friends had promised to send a letter up the chimney to remind him.

Christmas Eve came at last. Piccola's mother hurried home from her work; they had their little supper of soup and bread, and soon it was bedtime, — time to get ready for Santa Claus. But oh! Piccola remembered then for the first time that the children had told her she must hang up her stocking, and she hadn't any, and neither had her mother.

How sad, how sad it was! Now Santa Claus would come, and perhaps be angry because he couldn't find any place to put the present.

The poor little girl stood by the fireplace, and the big tears began to run down her cheeks. Just then her mother called to her, "Hurry, Piccola; come to bed." What should she do? But she stopped crying, and tried to think; and in a moment she remembered her wooden shoes, and ran off to get one of them. She put it close to the chimney, and said to herself, "Surely Santa Claus will know what it's there for. He will know I haven't any stockings, so I gave him the shoe instead."

Then she went off happily to her bed, and was asleep almost as soon as she had nestled close to her mother's side.

The sun had only just begun to shine, next morning, when Piccola awoke. With one jump she was out on the floor and running toward the chimney. The wooden shoe was lying where she had left it, but you could never, never guess what was in it.

Piccola had not meant to wake her mother,

"SEE THE PRESENT SANTA CLAUS BROUGHT ME'" (page 163)

but this surprise was more than any little girl could bear and yet be quiet; so she danced to the bed with the shoe in her hand, calling, "Mother, mother! look, look! see the present Santa Claus brought me!"

Her mother raised her head and looked into the shoe. "Why, Piccola," she said, "a little chimney swallow nestling in your shoe? What a good Santa Claus to bring you a bird!"

"Good Santa Claus, dear Santa Claus!" cried Piccola; and she kissed her mother and kissed the bird and kissed the shoe, and even threw kisses up the chimney, she was so happy.

When the birdling was taken out of the shoe, they found that he did not try to fly, only to hop about the room; and as they looked closer, they could see that one of his wings was hurt a little. But the mother bound it up carefully, so that it did not seem to pain him, and he was so gentle that he took a drink of water from a cup, and even ate crumbs and seeds from Piccola's hand. She was a proud little girl when she took her Christmas present to show the children in the garden. They had

had a great many gifts, — dolls that could say
"mamma," bright picture-books, trains of cars,
toy pianos; but not one of their playthings
was alive, like Piccola's birdling. They were
as pleased as she, and Rose hunted about the
house till she found a large wicker cage that
belonged to a blackbird she once had. She
gave the cage to Piccola, and the swallow
seemed to make himself quite at home in it at
once, and sat on the perch winking his bright
eyes at the children. Rose had saved a bag of
candies for Piccola, and when she went home
at last, with the cage and her dear swallow
safely inside it, I am sure there was not a
happier little girl in the whole country of
Italy.

THE CHILD AND THE WORLD.

I SEE a nest in a green elm-tree
With little brown sparrows, — one, two, three!
The elm-tree stretches its branches wide,
And the nest is soft and warm inside.
At morn, the sun, so golden bright,
Climbs up to fill the world with light;
It opens the flowers, it wakens me,
And wakens the birdies, — one, two, three.
And leaning out of my window high,
I look far up at the blue, blue sky,
And then far out at the earth so green,
And think it the loveliest ever seen, —
The loveliest world that ever was seen!

But by and by, when the sun is low,
And birds and babies sleepy grow,
I peep again from my window high,
And look at the earth and clouds and sky.
The night dew comes in silent showers,
To cool the hearts of thirsty flowers;

The moon comes out, — the slender thing,
A crescent yet, but soon a ring, —
And brings with her one yellow star;
How small it looks, away so far!
But soon, in the heaven's shining blue,
A thousand twinkle and blink at you,
Like a thousand lamps in the sky so blue.

And hush! a light breeze stirs the tree,
And rocks the birdies, — one, two, three.
What a beautiful cradle, that soft, warm nest!
What a dear little coverlid, mamma-bird's
    breast!
She's hugging them close to her, — tight, so
    tight
That each downy head is hid from sight;
But out from under her sheltering wings
Their bright eyes glisten, — the darling
    things!
I lean far out from my window's height
And say, "Dear, lovely world, good-night!

"Good-night, dear, pretty baby moon!
Your cradle you'll outgrow quite soon,
And then, perhaps, all night you'll shine,
A grown-up lady moon! — so fine

And bright that all the stars
Will want to light their lamps from yours.
Sleep sweetly, birdies, never fear,
For God is always watching near!
And you, dear, friendly world above,
The same One holds us in His love:
Both you so great, and I so small,
Are safe, — He sees the sparrow's fall, —
The dear God watcheth over all!"

WHEN I WAS A LITTLE GIRL.

OUR FROGGERY.

"Turn back observantly into your own youth, and awaken, warm, and vivify the eternal youth of your mind." — FROEBEL.

WHEN I was a little girl my sister and I lived in the country. She was younger than I, and the dearest, fattest little toddlekins of a sister you ever knew. She always wanted to do exactly as I did, so that I had to be very careful and do the right things; for if I had been naughty she would surely have been naughty too, and that would have made me very sad.

As we lived in the country we had none of the things to amuse us that city children have. We could n't walk in crowded streets and see people and look in at beautiful shop-windows, or hear the street-organs play and see the monkeys do tricks; we could n't go to dancing school, nor to children's parties, nor to the circus to see the animals.

But we had lovely plays, after all.

In the spring we hunted for mayflowers, and sailed boats in the brooks, and gathered fluffy pussy-willows. We watched the yellow dandelions come, one by one, in the short green grass, and we stood under the maple-trees and watched the sap trickle from their trunks into the great wooden buckets; for that maple sap was to be boiled into maple sugar and syrup, and we liked to think about it. In the summer we went strawberrying and blueberrying, and played "hide and coop" behind the tall yellow haycocks, and rode on the top of the full haycarts.

In the fall we went nutting, and pressed red and yellow autumn leaves between the pages of our great Webster's Dictionary; we gathered apples, and watched the men at work at the cider-presses, and the farmers as they threshed their wheat and husked their corn. And in the winter we made snow men, and slid downhill from morning till night when there was any snow to slide upon, and went sleighing behind our dear old horse Jack, and roasted apples in the ashes of the great open fire.

But one of the things we cared for most was our froggery, and we used to play there for hours together in the long summer days.

Perhaps you don't know what a froggery is; but you do know what a frog is, and so you can guess that a froggery is a place where frogs live. My little sister and I used at first to catch the frogs and keep them in tin cans filled with water; but when we thought about it we saw that the poor froggies could n't enjoy this, and that it was cruel to take them away from their homes and make them live in unfurnished tin houses. So one day I asked my father if he would give us a part of the garden brook for our very own. He laughed, and said, "Yes," if we would n't carry it away.

Our garden was as large as four or five city blocks, and a beautiful silver-clear brook flowed through it, turning here and there, and here and there breaking into tinkling little waterfalls, and dropping gently into clear, still pools.

It was one of these deep, quiet pools that we chose for our froggery. It was almost hidden on two sides by thick green alder-bushes, so that it was always cool and pleasant there, even on the hottest days.

My father put pieces of fine wire netting into the water on each of the four sides of the pool, and so arranged them that we could slip those on the banks up and down as we pleased. Whenever we went there we always took away the side fences, and sat flat down upon the smooth stones at the edges of the brook and played with the frogs.

Here we used to watch our gay young polliwogs grow into frogs, one leg at a time coming out at each "corner" of their fat wriggling bodies. We kept two great bull-frogs, — splendid bass singers both of them, — that had been stoned by naughty small boys, and left for dead by the roadside. We found them there, bound up their broken legs and bruised backs, and nursed them quite well again in one corner of the froggery that we called the hospital. In another corner was the nursery, and here we kept all the tiniest frogs; though we always let them out once a day to play with the older ones, for fear that they never would learn anything if they were kept entirely to themselves.

One of our great bull-frogs grew so strong and well, after being in the hospital for a while, that he jumped over the highest of the wire fences, which was two feet higher than any frog ever was known to jump, so our hired man said, — jumped over and ran away. We called him the "General," because he was the largest of our frogs and the oldest, we thought. (He had n't any gray hairs, but he was very much wrinkled.) We were sorry to lose the General, and could n't think why he should run away, when we gave him such good things to eat and tried to make him so happy. My father said that perhaps his home was in a large pond, some distance off, where there were so many hundred frogs that it was quite a gay city life for them, while the froggery was in a quiet brook in our quiet old garden. (If I were a frog, it seems to me I should like such a home better than a great noisy stagnant pond near the road, where I should be frightened to death half a dozen times a day but there is no accounting for tastes!)

"WE WERE SORRY TO LOSE THE GENERAL" (page 172)

But what do you think? After staying away for three days and nights the General came back safe and sound! We knew it was our own beloved General, and not any common stranger-frog, because there was the scar on his back where the boys had stoned him. My little sister thought that perhaps the General was born in Lily Pad Pond, on the other side of the village, and only went back to get a sight of the pond lilies, which were just in full bloom. If that was so, I cannot blame the General; for snow-white pond lilies, with their golden hearts and the green frills round their necks, are the loveliest things in the world, as they float among their shiny pads on the surface of the pond. Did you ever see them?

All our frogs had names of their own, of course, and we knew them all apart, although they looked just alike to other people. There was Prince Pouter, Brownie, and Goldilegs; Bright-Eye, Chirp, and Gray Friar; Hop-o'-my-Thumb, Croaker, Baby Mine, Nimblefoot, Tiny Tim, and many others.

We were so afraid that our frogs would n't like the froggery better than any other place in the brook that we gave them all the pleasures we could think of. They always had plenty of fat juicy flies and water-bugs for their dinners, and after a while we put some silver shiners and tiny minnows into the pool, so that they would have fishes to play with as well as other frogs. You know you do not always like to play with other children; sometimes you like kittens and dogs and birds better.

Then we gave our frogs little vacations once in a while. We tied a long soft woolen string very gently round one of their hind legs, fastened it to a twig of one of the alder-bushes, and let them take a long swim and make calls on all their friends.

We had a singing-school for them once a week. It was very troublesome, for they did n't like to stand in line a bit, and it is quite useless to try and teach a class in singing unless the scholars will stand in a row or keep in some sort of order. We used to put a nice little board across the pool, and then try to get the frogs to sit quietly in line during their lesson. The General behaved quite nicely, and really got into the spirit of the thing, so that he was a splendid example for the head of the class. Then we used to put Myron W. Whitney next in line, on account of his beautiful bass voice. We named him after a gentleman who had once sung in our church, and I hope if he ever heard of it he did n't mind, for the frog was really a credit to him. Myron W. Whitney behaved nearly as well as the General, but we could never get him to sing unless we held the class just before bedtime, and then the little frogs were so sleepy that they kept tumbling out of the singing-school into the pool. That was the trouble with them all; they never could quite see the difference between *school* and *pool*. It seems to me they must have known it was very slight after all.

Towards the end of the summer we had trained them so well that once in a long while we could actually get them all still at once, and all facing the right way as they sat upon that board. Oh! it was a beautiful sight, and worth any amount of trouble and work! Twenty-one frogs in a row, all in fresh green suits, with clean white shirt fronts, washed every day. The General and Myron W.

Whitney always looked as if they were bursting with pride, and as they were too fat and lazy to move, we could generally count upon their good behavior.

We thought that if we could only get them to look down into the pool, which made such a lovely looking-glass, and just see for once what a beautiful picture they made, — sitting so straight and still, and all so nicely graded as to size, — they would like it better and do it a little more willingly.

We thought, too, the baby frogs would be ashamed, when they looked in the glass, to see that while the big frogs stayed still of their own free will, *they* had to be held down with forked sticks. But we could never discover that they were ashamed.

So when everything was complete my little sister used to "let go" of the baby frogs (for, as I said, she had to hold them down while we were forming the line), and I would begin the lesson. Sometimes they would listen a minute, and then they would begin their pranks. They would insist on playing leap-frog, which is a very nice game, but not appropriate for school. Tiny Tim would jump from the foot of the class straight over all the others on to Myron W. Whitney's back. Baby Mine would try to get between Croaker and Goldilegs, where there was n't any room. Nimblefoot would twist round on the board and turn his back to me, which was very impolite, as I was the teacher. Finally, Hop-o'-my-Thumb would go splash into the pool, and all the rest, save the good old General, would follow him, and the lesson would end. I suppose you have heard frogs singing just after sunset, when you were going to bed? Some people think the big bull-frogs say, "*Jugo'rum! Jugo'rum! Jugo'rum!*" But I don't think this is at all likely, as the frogs never drink anything but water in their whole lives.

We used to think that some of the frogs said, "*Kerchug! Kerchug!*" and that the largest one said, "*Gotacrumb! Gotacrumb! Gotacrumb!*" Perhaps you can't make it sound right, but if you listen to the frogs you can very soon do it.

We thought the frogs in our froggery the very best singers in all the country round. After our mother had tucked us in our little beds and kissed us good-night, she used to open the window, that we might hear the chirping and humming and kerchugging of our frogs down in the dear old garden.

As we wandered dreamily off into Sandman's Land, the very last sound we heard was the cheerful chorus of our baby frogs, and the deep bass notes of Myron W. Whitney and the old General.

FROEBEL'S BIRTHDAY.

"The whole future efficiency of man is seen in the child as a germ." — FROEBEL.

On this day, children, the twenty-first of April, we always remember our dear Froebel; for it was his birthday.

We bring flowers and vines to hang about his picture, we sing the songs and play the games he loved the best, and we remember the story of his life. We thank him all day long; for he made the kindergarten for us, he invented these pretty things that children love to do, he thought about all the pleasant work and pleasant play that make the kindergarten such a happy place.

On this very day, more than a hundred years ago, the baby Froebel came to his happy father and mother. He was a little German baby, like Elsa's brother and Fritz's little sister, and when he began to talk his first words were German ones.

But the dear mother did not stay long with her little Friedrich, for she died when he was not a year old, and he was left a very sad and lonely baby. His father was a busy minister, who had sermons to write, and sick people to see, and unhappy people to comfort, from one end of the week to the other, and he had no time to attend to his little son; so Friedrich was left to the housemaid, who was too busy herself to care for him properly. She was often so hurried that she was obliged to shut him up in a room alone, to keep him out of her way, and then it was very hard work for the child to amuse himself.

The only window in this room looked out on a church that workmen were repairing, and Friedrich often watched these men, and tried to do just as they did. He took all the small pieces of furniture, and piled one on top of the other to make a big, big church, like the one outside; but the chairs and stools did not fit each other very well, and soon the church would come tumbling about his head. When Froebel grew to be a man, he remembered this, and made the building blocks for us, so that we might make fine, tall churches and houses as often as we liked.

Froebel's home was surrounded by other buildings, and was close to the great church I told you about. There were fences and hedges all around the house, and at the back there were sloping fields, stretching up a high hill.

When the little boy grew old enough to walk, he played in the garden alone, a great deal of the time; but he was not allowed to go outside at all, and never could get even a glimpse of the world beyond. He could only see the blue sky overhead, and feel the fresh wind blowing from the hills.

His father had no time for him, his mother was dead, and I think perhaps he would have died himself, for very sadness and lonesomeness, if it had not been for his older brothers. Now and then, when they were at home, they played and talked with him, and he grew to love them very dearly indeed.

When Friedrich was four years old, his father brought the children a new mother, and for a time the little boy was very happy. The mother was quite kind at first; and now Froebel had some one to walk with in the garden, some one to talk with in the daytime and to tuck him in his little bed at night. But by and by, when a baby boy came to the new mother, she had no more room in her heart for poor Friedrich, and he was more miserable than ever. He tried to be a good boy, but no one seemed to understand him, and he was often blamed for naughty things he had not done, and was never praised or loved.

When he had learned to read he was sent to school, though not with other boys, for his father thought it better for him to be with girls. The school was pleasant and quiet, and Friedrich liked the teacher very much. Every morning the children read from the Bible, and learned sweet songs and hymns which the little boy remembered all his days.

The life at home grew no happier, as Friedrich grew older; indeed, he seemed to be more in the way and to get into trouble more often.

When he was ten years old his uncle came to visit them, and seeing Friedrich so unhappy, and fearing he would not grow up a good boy unless some one cared for him, the good uncle asked to be allowed to take the child home with him to live.

Now, at last, Friedrich had five happy years!

His uncle lived in a pretty town on the banks of a sparkling little river. Everything was pleasant in the house, and Friedrich went to school with forty boys of his own age. He jumped and ran with them in the playgrounds, he learned to play all kinds of games, and he was happy everywhere, — at school, at home, at church, playing or working.

When these five pleasant years had gone by, Froebel had finished school, and now he must decide what he would do to earn his living. He had always loved flowers, since the days when he played all alone in his father's garden, and he liked to be out-of-doors and to see things growing; so he made up his mind to be a surveyor, like our George Washington, you know, and to learn, besides, how to take care of trees and forests.

He studied and worked very hard at these things, and gained a great deal of knowledge about flowers and plants and trees and rocks.

By and by he left this work and went to college, where he studied a long time and grew to be very wise indeed. There were numbers of things he had learned to do: he could measure land, take care of woods, and draw maps; he could make plans of houses, and show men how to build them; he knew all about fine stones and minerals, and could sort and arrange them; but he found, at last, that there was nothing in the world he liked so well as teaching, for he loved children very much, and he liked to be with them.

When Froebel was a grown man, thirty years old, a great war broke out in Germany, and he went away to fight for his country; like our George Washington again, you see. He marched away with the soldiers, and fought bravely for a year; and then the war was over, and he went back to his quiet work again.

For the rest of his life Froebel went on teaching all kinds of people, — boys and men, and young girls and grown-up women; but he never was quite happy or satisfied till he thought of teaching tiny children, just like you.

He remembered very well how sad and miserable he was when a little boy, with no one to love him, nobody to play with, and nothing to do; so he thought of the kindergarten, where there are pleasant playmates, pretty work, happy play for everybody, and teachers who love little children.

He was an old man when he thought of the kindergarten; but he was never too old to play with children, and people who went to his country home used to see him, with the little ones about him, playing the Pigeon House, or the Wheel, or the Farmer, or some of the games he made for us.

He was often very poor, and he worked very hard all his life; but he did not care for this at all, if he could help other people and make children happy. And when, at last, it was time for him to die, and to go back to God, who sent him to us, he was quiet and happy through all his sickness, and almost the last words he said were about the flowers he loved so well, and about God who had been so good to him.

So this is the reason, little ones, that we keep Froebel's birthday every year, — because we want you to remember all he did for little children, and to learn to love him just as he loved you.

"Come, let us live with our children; so shall their lives bring peace and joy to us; so shall we begin to be, and to become wise."
— FROEBEL.

www.ingramcontent.com/pod-product-compliance
Lightning Source LLC
Chambersburg PA
CBHW021734220426
43662CB00008B/848